FABULOUS FOOD BY MAIL

THE ESSENTIAL SOURCEBOOK

Lexington College

310 S. Peoria St. Ste. 512
Chicago, Il 60607 3534

Phone 312-226-6294
Fax   312-226-6405

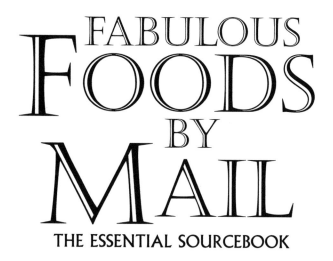

FABULOUS FOODS BY MAIL

THE ESSENTIAL SOURCEBOOK

REBECCA GRAY

WILLOW CREEK PRESS

Published in 1997 by Willow Creek Press
P.O. Box 147
Minocqua, WI 54548

For information on other Willow Creek Press titles,
call 1-800-850-WILD

Many of the entries in this book were submitted by the vendors via the internet and compiled in a database. Therefore, if any addresses are incorrect, Willow Creek Press cannot be held responsible. If brought to the attention of Willow Creek Press, inaccuracies will be corrected in future editions.

Library of Congress Cataloging-in-Publication Data
Gray, Rebecca
    Fabulous Foods by Mail / By Rebecca Gray
    ISBN 1-57223-123-8

Design by Heather M. McElwain

Printed in the United States of America

TABLE OF CONTENTS

DEDICATION

To Rick Sullivan and Jim Faughnan

And to all the Federal Express and United Parcel Service delivery people who not only do their jobs well, but know the meaning of good, old-fashioned "service with a smile." You are what makes fabulous food by "mail" the best.

ACKNOWLEDGEMENTS

With great appreciation to Tom Petrie, Publisher of Willow Creek Press, who continues to reach far beyond the usual realm of publisher; first as mentor and friend and now even as the mastermind for this wonderful sourcebook. May this near idyllic relationship last for many years. To Heather McElwain whose great sense of design and organization have made this not just a pretty book but a very "user-friendly" tool as well. She's fast at it, too! And Ed Gray, without whose computer knowledge this book would have been virtually impossible to compile. My thanks also to Ed, Will, Hope, Sam, Sam's five roommates at Ohio State University, friends Nadia, Greg and Alex Gorman and Michael and Virginia Beahan for finishing the sample food after I'd completed testing; it saved me from at least ten additional pounds.

And most importantly my thanks to the people in the food companies represented here. Without their passion to produce great products there would be absolutely no reason for this book to exist.

Other books by **Rebecca Gray**

Eat Like a Wild Man: The Ultimate Fish and Game Cookbook —
Sports Afield/Willow Creek Press (July 1997)

When Fishermen Cook Fish — Willow Creek Press (1996)

Gray's Fish Cookbook — Gray's Sporting Journal Press (1986)

Gray's Wild Game Cookbook — Gray's Sporting Journal Press (1983)

INTRODUCTION

There is very nearly a food revolution going on and it's happening right at our front doors, right in our mail boxes. Although ordering food through the mail is not a new activity — after all companies like Harry and David have been shipping their pears around the country for over 61 years — mail-ordered food is taking on new life and new reason for being.

In 1993, the last year that statistics on the subject were available, mail-order food companies took nearly eight million orders, a 40% increase over the previous year which was already at a $1.2 billion level!

Certainly such growth is at least partially precipitated by the changes in our "mail" system. Our first Postmaster General, Ben Franklin, may have actually created the mail order business by mailing his 1744 book catalog. Although we still order lots of books by "mail," the chosen mode of delivery is not the U.S. postal system; it is now Federal Express and United Parcel Service. Very few of the samples I tested actually came through the mail; Jim, my UPS delivery man, and I have become great buddies. In the old, slow mail-order food days, U.S. mail primarily delivered the relatively less perishable items like jams, jelly and fruitcakes and that was all. Now FedEx can bring me a Legal Seafood lobster boil, complete with clams and covered in seaweed that came from the ocean the day before.

What is intriguing about mail-order food since the advent of near instant delivery is that it is actually arriving fresher that what we purchase in the grocery store. Jasch Hamilton at Diamond Organics pointed out that the California baby carrots and zucchini that I received from him (picked that morning and overnighted to me) would have spent many days in trucks and warehouses and then potentially many more days in the back of the supermarket before getting stocked on the shelves. And if freshness of mail-order food is potentially superior to the supermarket's then so must be that linked characteristic: quality. Better quality comes not only from greater freshness but from access to the expert growing or production techniques; to the appropriate region of the country, too. It I want a perfectly dry-aged, ribeye steak, it's nice to be able to purchase it from a Midwestern cattle man whose family has been dry-aging beef since the 1930s, such as Dreisbach's.

Ten or twelve years ago FedEx and UPS started the speedy food delivery revolution thereby enhancing the freshness and quality of food by mail; now there's a second transformation affecting the very ease of food selection. For some time now shopping by mail has had the attribute of efficiency, particularly when it came to gift giving. One phone call and the gift was purchased and delivered with no trips to the mall, post office or perspiration spent on wrapping or walking. We now benefit more with the advent of the internet; we can browse quite handily and with tremendous depth. In researching this book I found over 1,000 food company websites through one search engine alone. The sites told me everything from the family history of the company owners to recipes and suggestions on how best to use their product. I could read about Rubye Jean and Raymond Bland and their Vidalia onion farm or the young chef at the Sacher Hotel who created the now-famous torte for the Austrian king; peruse literally hundreds of coffee company sites and choose the specific Puerto Rican estate from which I want my beans. I had options, complete information and could order it all without leaving my computer.

In the end, overnight delivery and the internet have provided greater satisfaction in our cooking and eating. Whether it be obtaining better prepared foods or in preparing foods ourselves with better ingredients; it's happening by mail. The current American passion to focus on healthy eating and expedient sophisticated cooking suits what mail-order food can deliver. Why waste your time on preparing a tiramisù if you don't have good mascarpone? Why spend your once-a-week steak apportionment on the select cut from the supermarket when you can have prime in your mailbox? In our search for new and unusual taste sensations, in our indulgence in the patchwork of food that is the American cuisine, and in our quest to become more connected with what it is we eat; it is the food from around the world, the food we learn about, that most appeals.

What I can say about the nearly 400 food companies I dealt with in the creation of this book is that they all have a very consistent and common characteristic: They are genuinely proud of the product they produce; calling to talk so cheerfully about it, sending more than just the tiny sample I suggested (I'm lucky I didn't gain 50 pounds) and wanting to ensure satisfaction. I think the food people here like what they do everyday and it shows. Next time it will be easier. I believe there is a need for this book; it provides such a reader/consumer service to a truly explosive market, that an updated sourcebook for mail-order food will be bigger and better than ever. And in an effort to start right now on creating that bigger and better version, please send me names and addresses of great mail-order food companies not already listed here. Whether it is your own company or one whose products you savor, let me hear about it: Rebecca Gray, P.O. Box 69, Lyme, NH 03768 or e-mail: Graybooks@aol.com

But for now; here, as near as your mailbox and from those who know the art of incredible edibles, is a wonderful cornucopia of fabulous food; may you enjoy it.

— Rebecca Gray

KEY

Food is very personal; what constitutes good food is very much a matter of taste. This is the reason I have not rated the foods in the book. There is nothing here which suggests that a particular smoked salmon is The Best. The best is dependent on the evening, the wine, the guests, the memory of a salmon fishing trip to Scotland, the temperature of the water the salmon swam in, the temperature of the smoke or the grill or a thousand other ingredients that participate in making something delicious. And every person is different; if you doubt this ask ten people their opinion of a fruitcake. The comments I have made on sampled products are a starting point. So much fabulous food; so little time: you might as well start from some reference point. At very least I can say I have tried a lot of foods, both in my food-writing career and for this book. I feel confident that you will not be disappointed with anything on my "must try" list. Although the selections are riddled with my own biases (there seems to be a lot of chocolate on the list) and sometimes the items are chosen not just for taste but as much for their pizzazz. Please note, also, that an unsampled item means just that, and it should not hold any kind of stigma. There were many very valid reasons that samples could not be provided, product seasonality being but one of those reasons.

Many upstanding companies did not make it into the book; those that I couldn't find or that I contacted and who didn't respond (Only 260 food companies replied to my nearly 900 e-mails requesting participation). Of course, I'm not certain why they didn't respond but there is still some mistrust of the internet and who is behind all those slashes, dots and coms. And, too, there is the big "I" word (inertia) which says something about a company's marketing skills but nothing about its ability to produce a tasty product.

 Sampled Selection

 "Must Try" Selection

 Good Gift

 Subcategory Selection

MUST TRY LIST

BEVERAGES

Coffees, teas, wines, beers and spirits; also beverage clubs.

1-800-MICROBREW

3053 Filmore, Suite 242
San Francisco, CA 94123
PHONE (800) MICROBREW; FAX (415) 666-0300
WEB SITE www.800microbrew.com
E-MAIL member@800microbrew

SIGNATURE PRODUCT **Microbrew beer**

ADDITIONAL PRODUCTS Twelve bottles of specialty, sometimes hard-to-find, hand-crafted microbrew delivered to your home or office each month, along with a copy of our informative, fun-to-read newsletter

All Hawaii Coffee

480 Kenolio Road #5-206
Kihei, HI 96753
PHONE (800) 565-2088; FAX (808) 875-4858
WEB SITE http://www.mauigateway.com/~coffee/
E-MAIL coffee@mauigateway.com

SIGNATURE PRODUCT **Gourmet Hawaii Coffee**

NEWEST PRODUCT Hawaiian Macadamia Nuts
COMMENTS *Kona coffee is like none other in the world and this Kona is the real thing; very, very good*

Annie & I Gourmet Coffee and Teas

P.O. Box 315
Perris, CA 92571
PHONE (909) 940-1184
WEB SITE   http://www.pe.net/~anniei/index.html
E-MAIL   anniei@pe.net

SIGNATURE PRODUCT   *Private blends of fine coffee and teas*

Armeno Coffee Roasters

75 Otis Street
Northborough, MA 01532
PHONE (800)ARMENO; FAX (508) 393-2818
WEB SITE   www.armeno.com
E-MAIL   beans@armeno

SIGNATURE PRODUCT   *Estate coffee*

ADDITIONAL PRODUCTS   Armeno offers 60 estate varietals of coffee
    from all over the world. In-direct, slow roasting of the coffee beans
    and freshness contribute to the quality of the coffee
COMMENTS   *This coffee is truly different and outstanding. I particularly liked
    the Zambian AA and the Celebres Kalossi. This coffee is on my "must try" list.*

Aroma Borealis

#211 10130 103 St.
Edmonton, Alberta CANADA T5J 3N9
PHONE (800) 469-8842; FAX (403) 944-9604
WEB SITE   http://www.tgx.com/coffee
E-MAIL   coffee@oanet.com

SIGNATURE PRODUCT   *Copenhagen Breakfast Blend (Gourmet Coffee)*

ADDITIONAL PRODUCTS   We carry over 60 varieties of gourmet coffee
    & teas.

Bamboo Tea House

221 Yale Avenue
Claremont, CA 91711
PHONE (909) 626-7668; FAX (909) 398-1486
WEB SITE www.bambooteas.com
E-MAIL bambootea@sprintmail.com

SIGNATURE PRODUCT *Teas*

NEWEST PRODUCT Shan tea from Viet Nam
ADDITIONAL PRODUCTS Green teas, oolong, black teas, herb teas, flavored teas, tea accessories

Barrington Coffee Roasting Company Inc.

955 South Main Street
Great Barrington, MA 01230
PHONE (800) 528-0998; FAX (413) 528-0614
WEB SITE http://www.barringtoncoffee.com
E-MAIL info@barringtoncoffee.com

SIGNATURE PRODUCT **Freshly Roasted Arabica Coffees**

NEWEST PRODUCT French Roast Costa Rican (San Antonio Estate)
ADDITIONAL PRODUCTS Over forty estate coffee varietals

Barry's Tea

P.O. Box 843
Babylon, NY 11702
PHONE (800) 422-7516; FAX (516) 422-6740
WEB SITE http://www.barrystea.com
E-MAIL barrys@specdata.com

SIGNATURE PRODUCT **Barry's Gold Blend and Green Label Teas - Loose and in bags!**

NEWEST PRODUCT Barry's Classic Blend Tea in collector tin

Beer Across America

55 Albrecht Drive
Lake Bluff, IL 60044
PHONE (880) 854-BEER; FAX (847) 604-8821
WEB SITE   www.beeramerica.com

SIGNATURE PRODUCT   *Mail-order microbrews*

NEWEST PRODUCT   Cigars
ADDITIONAL PRODUCTS   Wine, premium wine, gourmet coffee
COMMENTS   *The coffee, beer and wine sampled from BAA were all just terrific and not brands I would normally choose, which is what makes clubs like this fun. I particularly liked the Goose Island Honker's Ale. Big selection of beer!*

Bewley Irish Imports

1130 Greenhill Road
West Chester, PA 19380
PHONE (610) 696-2682; FAX (610) 344-7618

SIGNATURE PRODUCT   *Bewley's of Ireland Teas*

NEWEST PRODUCT   Lakeshore Tipperary Pub Mustard
ADDITIONAL PRODUCTS   Alexander's Irish Whiskey Marmalades; Ballymaloe Country Relish; Bewley's teas, coffees, and cakes; Hogans Soda Bread Mix; Irish Dawn Herbal Teas; Lakeshore Mustards; McCanns Irish Oatmeal; Shamrock Preserves; Wilson's English Food
COMMENTS   *The tea was lovely; full of heft and flavor.*

Blue Zebu Fine Coffee

2820 Camino Del Rio South, Suite 204 A
San Diego, CA 92108
PHONE (619) 645-8955; FAX (619) 296-6578
WEB SITE   www.bluezebu.com
E-MAIL   bluezebu@cts.com

SIGNATURE PRODUCT   *Blue Zebu Guatemalan coffee*

ADDITIONAL PRODUCTS   The Guatemalan coffee beans are bagged in six different Mayan fabric pouches.

COMMENTS   *Very distinctive item; the coffee is highly flavorful, but not too hefty. The Mayan fabric sack is very nice.*

▦ *Boehms Chocolates*
1101 Supermall Way #1332
Auburn, WA 98001
PHONE (206) 735-1994; FAX (206) 735-1911
WEB SITE   www.forsuccess.com/chocolate/boehms
E-MAIL   boehms@wolfenet.com

▦ *Bountiful Baskets*
2117 Concord Pike
Wilmington, DE 19803
PHONE (888) 737-6727; FAX (302) 658-7664
WEB SITE   www.coffeecreations.com

The Brew Tour
P.O. Box 471
Oregon City, Oregon 97045
PHONE (800) 660-TOUR

SIGNATURE PRODUCT   **Microbrew of the month club**

ADDITIONAL PRODUCTS   Unusual beers, from Cowboy, Red Lady and New Amsterdam to Bridgeport Blue Heron — 12 bottles a month of unique and hard-to-find beers arrive at your door

▦ *The British Gourmet*
45 Wall Street
Madison, CT 06443
PHONE (800) 842-6674; FAX (203) 245-3477
WEB SITE   www.thebritishshoppe.com
E-MAIL   gourmet@thebritisheshoppe.com

Brown & Jenkins Trading Co.

91 Ethan Allen Drive, P.O. Box 2306
Burlington, VT 05407-2306
PHONE (800) 456-5282; FAX (800) 888-5282
WEB SITE www.brownjenkins.com
E-MAIL coffee@brownjenkins.com

SIGNATURE PRODUCT **French roasted gourmet coffees**

ADDITIONAL PRODUCTS Many different coffees from all over the
world, different flavors and special roasts; decaffeinated, both
European and Swiss style, whole bean or ground available.
COMMENTS *I asked to test their Columbian Supremo which is my standard
morning brew; but ended up enjoying their Vermont blend as well or better!*

Cafe Rico

Caparra Heights Station, P.O. Box 11959
San Juan, PR 00922
PHONE (787) 782-0620; FAX (787) 793-8177
WEB SITE www.caferico.com
E-MAIL info@caferico.com

SIGNATURE PRODUCT **Puerto Rican Coffee**

NEWEST PRODUCT Cafe Rico Light Coffee (50% decaffeinated)
ADDITIONAL PRODUCTS Cafe Rico Espresso, Cafe Rico Decaffeinated
COMMENTS *All very nice and flavorful coffees; a distinctive taste which I like
in a coffee.*

The California Wine Club

2175 Goodyear Avenue, Suite #114
Ventura, CA 93003
PHONE (800) 777-4443; FAX (805) 650-4333
WEB SITE http://www.cawineclub.com
E-MAIL cawine@ix.netcom.com

SIGNATURE PRODUCT **Standard Wine Club Membership**

NEWEST PRODUCT Signature Series Wine Club Membership

ADDITIONAL PRODUCTS   Connoissuer's Series Wine Club
Membership; Reach Back & Try Program; case purchase discounts;
annual wine sales; gift giving for all occasions

COMMENTS   *This wine club is terrific if the sample they sent is indicative; I
would never have tried this wine (the label/name was a bit scary...Moonshine
Cabernet!) and it was absolutely great! On my "must try" list.*

Celebrations Wine Club
75 Pelican Way G1
San Rafael, CA 94901
PHONE (800) 700-6227

SIGNATURE PRODUCT   **California's most distinguished wine-of-the-
month club**

Chateau Gourmet Coffee
736 East Avenue
Brockport, NY 14420
PHONE (716) 637-3338; FAX (716) 637-9171
WEB SITE   www.alcasoft.com/chateau

SIGNATURE PRODUCT   Coffee

ADDITIONAL PRODUCTS   Twenty-two different coffees; 10 different
flavored coffee creamers; 10 flavored iced teas; 5 flavored tropical iced
teas; 14 flavored hot chocolates and more

The Joseph Cerniglia Winery
37 West Road
Bennington, VT 05201
PHONE (800) 639-1625; FAX (802) 442-4410
WEB SITE   www.thisisvermont.com/vtwines.html
E-MAIL   grgrryan@sover.net

SIGNATURE PRODUCT   **Vermont Wines**

The Coffee Mug

3405 Sweetwater Road, Suite 434
Lawrenceville, GA 30244
PHONE (770) 446-7138
WEB SITE www.coffeemug.com

SIGNATURE PRODUCT *Coffee*

ADDITIONAL PRODUCTS Many different types of gourmet coffee, tea,
cappuccino, and espresso. Also gift baskets that include customizing
options with many different novelty items.

Collandra, Inc.

2790 NW 104th Court
Miami, FL 33172
PHONE (800) 673-0532; FAX (305) 380-0859
WEB SITE www.caribplace.com/foods/trout.htm
E-MAIL colland@earthlink.net

Enoteca Wine Club

7121 Amarillo Drive
Charlotte, NC 28262
PHONE (800) 655-3429
WEB SITE www.mindspring.com/~enoteca

SIGNATURE PRODUCT **Wine club**

ADDITIONAL PRODUCTS Unusual and hard-to-find wines from around
the world. Two selections are delivered each month right to your door.

Heavenly Cheesecakes & Chocolates Inc.

1369 Ridgewood Avenue
Holly Hill, FL 32117
PHONE (904) 673-6670; FAX (904) 673-2367
WEB SITE www.heavenlycheesecakes.com
E-MAIL Heavenlycheesecakes@juno.com

Hogs Head Beer Cellars

620 S. Elm Street
Greensboro, NC 27406
PHONE (800) 795-BEER; FAX (910) 574-2739
WEB SITE   hogshead.com
E-MAIL   beerclub@hogshead.com

SIGNATURE PRODUCT   *Beer-of-the-Month Club*

ADDITIONAL PRODUCTS   Many hard-to-find and great microbrews
COMMENTS   *I really liked the Captain's Lager from Steamship Brewing Co.
It's difficult to find a really robust, good lager these days; this is one.*

Indiana Botanic Gardens

P.O. Box 5, Dept. FIIW
Hammond, IN 46325
PHONE (800) 644-8327; FAX (219) 947-4148
WEB SITE   www.botanichealth.com
E-MAIL   botanichealth@niia.net

SIGNATURE PRODUCT   *Gourmet spice basket*

NEWEST PRODUCT   Herbal tea basket
ADDITIONAL PRODUCTS   Green tea, Fenugreek tea, lecithin granules,
chamomile tea, etc.

Leavenworth Coffee Roasters

1038 Front Street
Leavenworth, WA 98826
PHONE (509) 548-1428; FAX (509) 548-8067
WEB SITE   http://www.chattercreek.com
E-MAIL   info@chattercreek.com

SIGNATURE PRODUCT   *Chatter Creek Coffee — over 25 different
roasts and blends*

Lion Coffee

P.O. Box 1300, Lock Box #47867
Honolulu, HI 96813-5204
PHONE (800) 338-8353; FAX (800) 972-0777
WEB SITE www.lioncoffee.com
E-MAIL lion@lioncoffee.com

SIGNATURE PRODUCT *Hawaiian coffee*

NEWEST PRODUCT Cafe Hawaii in medium and dark roasts
ADDITIONAL PRODUCTS We have 19 different gourmet coffee varieties; from Kona Gold Dark, Diamond Head Espresso to toasted coconut and chocolate macadamia nut.

Liquor By Wire

2835 N. Sheffield, Suite 409
Chicago, IL 60657
PHONE (800) 621-5150; FAX (773) 325-9576
WEB SITE www.lbw.com
E-MAIL lbw2835@aol.com

SIGNATURE PRODUCT *Gift liquors*

ADDITIONAL PRODUCTS World-wide gift delivery of wines, champagnes, spirits, gift baskets, and more

Louisiana French Market Online

4614 Tupello Street
Baton Rouge, LA 70808
PHONE (504) 928-1428; FAX (504) 774-4085
WEB SITE http://www.louisianafrenchmarket.com
E-MAIL service@louisianafrenchmarket.com

Mauna Loa Macadamia Nuts

6523 North Galena Road, P.O. Box 1772
Peoria, IL 61656
PHONE (800) 832-9993; FAX (309) 689-3893
WEB SITE www.maunaloa.com

MontBlanc Gourmet Hot Cocoa

425 South Cherry, Suite 630
Denver, CO 80222
PHONE (800) 877-3811; FAX (303) 399-1616
WEB SITE   www.montblancgourmet.com
E-MAIL   mtblanc@montblancgourmet.com

SIGNATURE PRODUCT   *MontBlanc Gourmet Hot Cocoa*

NEWEST PRODUCT   MontBlanc Gourmet Syrups
ADDITIONAL PRODUCTS   Chocolate swirls, iced mocha drinks, toppings, and cocoa in assorted containers
COMMENTS   *This cocoa is truly gourmet hot chocolate, it can stand up to being made with just water rather than milk and still tastes great. I recommend it highly.*

Only Gourmet

P.O. Box 2214
Orinda, CA 94563
PHONE (888) 413-6637; FAX (510) 531-4981
WEB SITE   http://www.onlygourmet.com
E-MAIL   alank@onlygourmet.com

Passport Wine Club

1201 Andersen Drive, Suite M
San Rafael, CA 94901
PHONE (800) 867-9463; FAX (415) 456-7737
WEB SITE   topwine.com
E-MAIL   topwine@aol.com

SIGNATURE PRODUCT   **Wine-of-the-Month Club**

POP 'N STUFF INC.

Broadway at the Beach, 1303 Celebrity Circle 125
Myrtle Beach, SC 29577
PHONE (800) 735-5440; FAX (803) 946-6813
WEB SITE   http://sccoast.net/popn/popnstuf/home.htm:
E-MAIL   popn@sccoast.net

Sam's Wines & Spirits
1720 N. Macey Street
Chicago, IL 60614
PHONE (800) 777-9137; FAX (312) 664-7037
WEB SITE www.sams.wine.com

SIGNATURE PRODUCT **Wines & spirits**

ADDITIONAL PRODUCTS Huge selection of wines from all over the world; beers, spirits, cigars, glasses and accessories. Gift baskets also available.

Schroeder's Bakeries Inc.
212 Forest Avenue, P.O. Box 183
Buffalo, NY 14213-0183
PHONE (800) 850-7763; FAX (716) 885-0369
WEB SITE www.schroedersbakery.com
E-MAIL bakery@schroedersbakery.com

Sherry-Lehmann
679 Madison Avenue
New York, NY 10021
PHONE (212) 838-7500; FAX (212) 838-9285

SIGNATURE PRODUCT **Wines and spirits from around the world**

ADDITIONAL PRODUCTS Selection of wine glasses and wine-related accessories.
CATALOG INFO They send out five catalogs annually.

Sierra Sunset
P.O. Box 525
Crugars, NY 10521
PHONE (800) 832-8990; FAX (914) 739-7541

Simpson & Vail

3 Quarry Rd., P.O. Box 765
Brookfield, CT 06804
PHONE (800) 282-TEAS; FAX (203) 775-0462
WEB SITE   www.svtea.com
E-MAIL   info@svtea.com

SIGNATURE PRODUCT   *Specialty teas*

NEWEST PRODUCT   El Rey chocolate (Venezuelan)
ADDITIONAL PRODUCTS   Tea brewing accessories, tea pots, tea cozies,
coffees, specialty food products

▦ Special Delivery

3820 Ohio Avenue, Suite 4
St. Charles, IL 60174
PHONE (800) 805-GIFT
WEB SITE   www.specialgift.com

Stash Tea

▯▮

P.O. Box 910
Portland, OR 97207
PHONE (800) 826-4218; FAX (503) 684-4424
WEB SITE   www.stashtea.com
E-MAIL   stash@stashtea.com

SIGNATURE PRODUCT   *Specialty teas*

NEWEST PRODUCT   Exotica
ADDITIONAL PRODUCTS   Traditional black teas; flavored and spiced
teas; herbal and green teas; and specialty iced teas. Over 100 blends,
plus tea accessories, tea gifts, and food items (tortes, cookies and
cake/muffin/tea, bread mixes) to accompany teas
CATALOG INFO   Lovely, enticing catalog
COMMENTS   *Loved their orange spiced tea, although I haven't hit a bad one of
theirs yet!*

Tasty Link Inc.
517 Lafayette Avenue
Wyckoff, NJ 07481
PHONE (201) 944-8021; FAX (201) 944-8183
WEB SITE http://www.websternet.com/tasty.html
E-MAIL sales@websternet.com

Thompson's Fine Teas

2062 South Delaware
San Mateo, CA 94403
PHONE (800) 830-8835; FAX (415) 572-9857
WEB SITE www.fineteas.com
E-MAIL info@fineteas.com

SIGNATURE PRODUCT **Fine loose leaf teas**

ADDITIONAL PRODUCTS Unusual and fine teas from around the
world; black, green and rare white tea
CATALOG INFO Beautiful presentation, quite pleasing to the senses.
Can I say almost sensual?
COMMENTS *Extraordinary. Beautiful and very different teas with sensation-
al flavor. On the "must try" list.*

Wine-Club.com

1340 El Camino Real
Belmont, CA 94002
WEB SITE http://www.wine-club.com
E-MAIL info@wine-club.com; order@wine-club.com

SIGNATURE PRODUCT **All Wines & Liquors**

Yauco Selecto Estate Coffee

595 Avenida Hostos
San Juan, PR 00918
PHONE (787) 782-0620; FAX (787) 767-8257
WEB SITE www.yscoffee.com
E-MAIL sales@yscoffee.com

SIGNATURE PRODUCT   *Yauco Estate Gourmet Coffee*

NEWEST PRODUCT   La Tahona, a selection of whole bean gourmet coffees

ADDITIONAL PRODUCTS   Flavored coffees: vanilla, hazelnut, chocolate mint

COMMENTS   *The Puerto Rican coffee is very distinct and very nice.*

BAKED GOODS

Desserts from cheesecakes to cookies. Also includes breads, muffins, fruitcake, and sweet bars.

 Allen Brothers — *The Great Steakhouse Steaks*™
3737 S. Halsted Street
Chicago, IL 60609
PHONE (800) 957-0111; FAX (800) 890-9146
WEB SITE http://www.allenbrothers.com
E-MAIL info@allenbrothers.com

Allspice Bakery
201 Greenfield Avenue
Ardmore, PA 19003-1205
PHONE (215) 629-1904; FAX (215) 629-9894
WEB SITE http://www.alspicebakery
E-MAIL allmuff@gim.net

SIGNATURE PRODUCT **Lowfat & nonfat muffins & scones**

NEWEST PRODUCT Glutten-free Muffins
ADDITIONAL PRODUCTS We also make lowfat & fat-free cookies, biscotti, as well as more traditional higher octane muffins and scones.
COMMENTS *These are very dense, flavorful muffins that could serve as your entire meal! Pretty tasty! Especially liked the blueberry.*

Atkins Unlimited Inc.
15510 Stony Creek Way
Noblesville, IN 46060
PHONE (800) 235-4039; FAX (317) 773-3766
WEB SITE http://criweb.com/atkins
E-MAIL Twwiese@aol.com

SIGNATURE PRODUCT **Old Fashioned Creamy Cheesecake**

NEWEST PRODUCT   Cheesecake Sampler
ADDITIONAL PRODUCTS   Atkins Unlimited offers more than 100 delicious desserts including cheesecakes, mousse cakes, roll cakes, layer cakes, eclair cakes and many other elegant desserts.
COMMENTS   *The Turtle Cheesecake was beyond decadence. Great desserts!*

▓ *Balducci's*
11-02 Queens Plaza South
Long Island City, NY 11101
PHONE (800) 225-3822; FAX (718) 786-4125
WEB SITE   www.balducci.com

▓ *Bewley Irish Imports*
1130 Greenhill Road
West Chester, PA 19380
PHONE (610) 696-2682; FAX (610) 344-7618

Big Betty's
P.O. Box 531
Glenorchy, Tasmania AUSTRALIA 07010
PHONE   (61) 36261-3296
FAX   (61) 36261-3296
WEB SITE   www.ozemail.com.au/~bbetty's
E-MAIL   bbettys@ozemail.com.au

SIGNATURE PRODUCT   *Big Betty's Gourmet Pudding*

NEWEST PRODUCT   Big Betty's Black Forest Gourmet Pudding
ADDITIONAL PRODUCTS   Taste of Tasmania gift box: A selection of fine Tasmanian gourmet foods, native treats and locally produced confectionary.
COMMENTS   *The "pudding" is actually a cake in a tin; and it is wonderful. My husband thinks it tastes like a cross between my chocolate cake and his Mama Gray's (grandmother). Very high praise and deserved, too!*

Bland Farms

P.O. Box 506-PG19
Glenndale, GA 30427
PHONE (800) 843-2542; FAX (912) 654-1330
WEB SITE   www.blandfarms.com

Blue Chip Cookies

100 First Street, Suite 2030
San Francisco, CA 94105
PHONE (800) 888-YUMM;   FAX (415) 546-9717
WEB SITE   www.bluechipcookies.com
E-MAIL   bcci@best.com

SIGNATURE PRODUCT   *White Chocolate Macadamia Cookie*

NEWEST PRODUCT   Blue Chip Coffee
ADDITIONAL PRODUCTS   We ship gift boxes and tins of freshly baked
   cookies anywhere in the continental United States: Chocolate chip,
   white chocolate macadamia nut, almond toffee chip, oatmeal raisin,
   brownies and more.
COMMENTS   *These are outstanding cookies. The white chocolate macadamia
   nut cookies were incredible.*

Brigitte's Brownies

120 Doyle Street
Doylestown, PA 18901
PHONE (888) 340-2040; FAX (215) 340-2040
WEB SITE   www.brigittesbrownie.com

SIGNATURE PRODUCT   *Belgian triple chocolate brownies*

NEWEST PRODUCT   Low-fat brownies
ADDITIONAL PRODUCTS   Nine varieties of brownies available in sheet-
   pans for home use or in elegant gift boxes.

The British Gourmet

45 Wall Street
Madison, CT 06443
PHONE (800) 842-6674; FAX (203) 245-3477
WEB SITE www.thebritishshoppe.com
E-MAIL gourmet@thebritisheshoppe.com

Cafe Beaujolais Bakery

961 Ukiah Street, P.O. Box 730
Mendocino, CA 95460
PHONE (800) 930-0443; FAX (707) 937-3656
WEB SITE www.cafebeaujolais.com
E-MAIL cafebeau@men.org

SIGNATURE PRODUCT *Panforte di Mendocina*

NEWEST PRODUCT Austrian Seed Cereal
ADDITIONAL PRODUCTS Pear barbecue sauce, pancake & waffle mix, hot chocolate mix, wild mendocino blackberry jam, chocolate-covered graham crackers
CATALOG INFO Funky
COMMENTS *Almond panforte di mendocino was very unusual and quite good dense cake that originally was created during the Middle ages — definitely worth a try.*

Central Italian Company

115-A Hanson Drive
St. Clairsville, OH 43950
PHONE (614) 695-2135; FAX (614) 699-0099
WEB SITE ourworld.compuserve.com/homepages/LUCIANO NARDONE/bis.htm
E-MAIL n848@earthlink.net

SIGNATURE PRODUCT *Biscotti Italiani*

NEWEST PRODUCT Amaretti Italiani
COMMENTS *Very nice biscotti.*

China Ranch Date Farm
#8 China Ranch Road
Tecopa, CA 92389
PHONE (760) 852-4415

Collin Street Bakery

401 W. Seventh Street
Corsicana, TX 75110
PHONE (903) 504-1896; FAX (903) 645-6767
WEB SITE   www.collinstreetbakery.com
E-MAIL   collin@airmail.net

SIGNATURE PRODUCT   *Fruitcake*

COMMENTS   *It's a fruitcake!*

Cookie Arrangements by Patti's Sweets 'n Strings
P.O. Box 3355
Enfield, CT 06082
PHONE (800) 383-2148; FAX (860) 741-7248
WEB SITE   http://idt.net/~knutf
E-MAIL   knutf@idt.net

SIGNATURE PRODUCT   *Personalized Cookie Arrangements*

ADDITIONAL PRODUCTS   All Cookie Arrangements are tailored for the
occasion.

Cookie Bouquets Inc.

6665-H Huntley Road
Columbus, OH 43229
PHONE (800) 233-2171; FAX (614) 841-3950
WEB SITE   http://www.cookiebouquets.com
E-MAIL   chips@cookiebouquets.com

SIGNATURE PRODUCT   *Bouquets made with chocolate chip cookies*

NEWEST PRODUCT   Seasonal bouquets. We're always changing and
adding

ADDITIONAL PRODUCTS   We have long stem arrangements. Bouquets arranged in baskets, mugs, vases, tins, novelty containers and mixed with silk flowers. We put assorted types of cookies in boxes or tins. We custom design arrangements

COMMENTS   *Not only is this a unique presentation but the cookies are great, too.*

The Cookie Connection
1160 South 11th Street
San Jose, CA 95112-2448
PHONE (408) 295-5718
WEB SITE   www.soupweb.com/cookie/
E-MAIL   pgoeltz@earthlink.net

SIGNATURE PRODUCT **Oatmeal, choc-chip, raisin banana cookies**

NEWEST PRODUCT   Oatmeal dried fruit banana cookie

Cookie Island Inc.
Somewhere off the Southampton Coast, or 745 Fifth Avenue, Suite 1701
New York, NY 10151
PHONE (888) 266-5434; FAX (718) 349-7985
E-MAIL   headcookie@worldnet.com

SIGNATURE PRODUCT   **Original Cookie Fit Box**

NEWEST PRODUCT   Passport Program

ADDITIONAL PRODUCTS   Love Box Exam Cram, Happy Holidays, Happy Birthday, Are you a Cookiehead (Tee Shirt), Wholesale cookies. We work from a three-cookie base, adding different nuts and chips; Chocolate Chip, Oatmeal Raisin, Peanut Butter. Also, we customize cookies.

Cookies For You
117 Main Street South
Minot, ND 58701
PHONE (800) 814-5334; FAX (701) 839-6560
WEB SITE   http://www.tradecorridor.com/cookies
E-MAIL   cnatc@minot.ndak.net

SIGNATURE PRODUCT *Cookies*

NEWEST PRODUCT Cookie Bouquets
ADDITIONAL PRODUCTS Cookie tins, cookie baskets, cookie boxes

Cushman's
3325 Forest Hill Boulevard
West Palm Beach, FL 33406
PHONE (800) 776-7575; FAX (800) 776-4329
E-MAIL cushman@aol.com

Daniel Weaver Company
15th Avenue & Weavertown Road, P.O. Box 525
Lebanon, PA 17042
PHONE (800) WEAVERS; FAX (717) 274-6103

Dessert of the Month

16805 S. Central Avenue
Carson, CA 90746
PHONE (800) 800-2253; FAX (310) 668-2148

SIGNATURE PRODUCT *Fudge cake*

ADDITIONAL PRODUCTS Desserts: bars, cookies, and cakes. A variety
 of gift baskets and monthly gift plans
COMMENTS *Wonderful chocolate fudge cake. So rich and delicious it should
 be able to satisfy even the worst chocaholic for . . . one month until the next
 dessert arrives.*

Diane's Gourmet Luxuries
11121 N. Rodney Parhan
Little Rock, AR 72212
PHONE (501) 224-2639; FAX (501) 224-8921
WEB SITE www.dianes-gourmet.com
E-MAIL diane@diane-gourmet.com

Fancy Fortune Cookies

6265 Coffman Road
Indianapolis, IN 46268
PHONE (317) 299-8900; FAX (317) 298-3690
WEB SITE www.svr.com/cookies/
E-MAIL fcookies@surf-ici.com

SIGNATURE PRODUCT   *Gourmet fortune cookies*

NEWEST PRODUCT   Giant 4" fortune cookie
ADDITIONAL PRODUCTS   Twelve different delicious flavors.
Customized messages for inside the cookies, great for gifts and business promotions.

▓ Foods of New York

66 Peconic Avenue
Medford, NY 11763
PHONE (800) HOTDOG-6; FAX (516) 654-9109
WEB SITE http://www.nyhotdog.com
E-MAIL steve@nyhotdog.com

FortuneGram

15204 W. 73rd Avenue
Golden, CO 80007
PHONE (800) 377-8476; FAX (303) 431-2068
WEB SITE http://www.fortunegram.com
E-MAIL sales@fortunegram.com

SIGNATURE PRODUCT   **GIANT Gourmet Fortune Cookies You Personalize**

NEWEST PRODUCT   GIANT Gourmet PartyGrams/ up to 10 messages inside
COMMENTS   *This is really a kick! My FortuneGram cookie came with the message "Good Luck on Your Book!" My mind is awhirl with what messages I could send in this good-tasting cookie.*

Gazin's
2910 Toulouse Street, P.O. Box 19221
New Orleans, LA 70119-0221
PHONE   (800) 262-6410; FAX (504) 827-5319

Gethsemani Farms

3642 Monks Road
Trappist, KY 40051
PHONE (502) 549-4138; FAX (502) 549-4124
WEB SITE   www.monks.org

SIGNATURE PRODUCT   **Trappist cheese**

NEWEST PRODUCT   Trappist Bourbon Fudge
ADDITIONAL PRODUCTS   Trappist Bourbon Fruitcake
COMMENTS   *The Brothers may say that they are best-known for their fine
cheeses (and they are good), but it is their fruitcake that is truly heavenly
and like none other. This is on the "must try" list.*

Golden Choice Foods
Junction 731 and Riverrun Road, P.O. Box 640
Lancaster, VA 22503
PHONE (800) 988-5181; FAX (804) 462-0131
WEB SITE   http:www.hey.net/users/golden
E-MAIL   golenchoice@hey.net

SIGNATURE PRODUCT   **Sugar Free Cake Mixes**

NEWEST PRODUCT   Sugar Free Low Fat Coconut Cookie Mix
ADDITIONAL PRODUCTS   Sugar-free gelatins, puddings, mousse,
whipped toppings and cookie mixes

GOODIES Express
6510 S. Xenon Street
Littleton, CO 80127
PHONE (888) 904-1923; FAX (303) 904-1921
WEB SITE   http://www.goodiesexpress.com
E-MAIL   lynnzy@goodiesexpress.com

SIGNATURE PRODUCT   *Amazing Edibles Delivered Nationwide Overnight*

NEWEST PRODUCT   Birthday Box

ADDITIONAL PRODUCTS   Cookies, brownies, candies, monthly care packages, corporate care packages, special holiday packaging

COMMENTS   *These were really good, partially because they were so fresh . . . and partially because they were just that good! I particularly liked the brownies.*

The Gourmet Padre
405 W. Cloverhurst Avenue
Athens, GA 30606
PHONE (800) 43-PADRE; FAX (706) 543-7557
WEB SITE   www/gourmet-padre.com
E-MAIL   gpadre@negia.com

Grandma's Bake Shoppe
201 South 5th Street, P.O. Box 457
Beatrice, NE 68310
PHONE (800) 228-4030; FAX (402) 223-4465

SIGNATURE PRODUCT   *Fruitcake*

ADDITIONAL PRODUCTS   Amaretto Fruit & Nut Cake, pineapple macadamia cake, chocolate cherry amaretto almond cake

COMMENTS   *It's a fruitcake!*

Great Food Online
2030 1st Avenue, 3rd Floor
Seattle, WA 98121
PHONE (800) 841-5984; FAX (206) 443-3314
WEB SITE   http://www.greatfood.com
E-MAIL   proprietor@greatfood.com

Heavenly Cheesecakes & Chocolates Inc.

1369 Ridgewood Avenue
Holly Hill, FL 32117
PHONE (904) 673-6670; FAX (904) 673-2367
WEB SITE www.heavenlycheesecakes.com
E-MAIL Heavenlycheesecakes@juno.com

SIGNATURE PRODUCT *Cheesecakes*

ADDITIONAL PRODUCTS Twenty-two varieties of cheesecakes; chocolate truffle cake; scratch carrot cake; chocolate banana cake; 3 varieties
of rum cakes; cookies; gift baskets; assorted candies and chocolates;
specialty coffees

Hotel Sacher Wien

Philharmonikerstrafe 4
A-1010 Wein AUSTRIA
PHONE (43-1) 51-450-0; FAX (43-1) 51-457-810
WEB SITE www.sacher.co.at/sacher
E-MAIL hotel@sacher.co.at

SIGNATURE PRODUCT *Original Sacher-Torten*

ADDITIONAL PRODUCTS Varying sizes of the original and very famous
Sacher torte. Delivered to the U.S. via DHL-parcel service within 3 to
6 working days
COMMENTS *Unsampled (unfortunately)*

International Brownie, Inc.

602 Middle Street
Weymouth, MA 02189
PHONE (617) 340-1588; FAX (617) 331-1900
WEB SITE www.internationalbrownie.com
E-MAIL brownies@ix.netcom.com

SIGNATURE PRODUCT *Gourmet brownie gift bundle*

NEWEST PRODUCT Sugar-free varieties
ADDITIONAL PRODUCTS Many varieties of brownies in a wide selec-

tion of gift boxes; from Almond Joy-ous, and Caribbean Butterscotch Delight to Praline Pecan and Peanut Butter Fudge

COMMENTS   *So many brownies, so little time! These are terrific; I especially liked the Naked Fudge.*

International Food Broker
80 Westchester Business Park
Armonk, NY 10504
PHONE (914) 273-5910; FAX (914) 273-9224
WEB SITE   http://www.imcworld.com/imperial
E-MAIL   petr@imcworld.com

SIGNATURE PRODUCT   **Imperial Torte**

Jubilations

Building 7, Suite 8, 1536 Gardner Boulevard
Columbus, MS 39702
PHONE (800) 530-7808; FAX (601) 329-1558
WEB SITE   http://www.tilc.com/jubilations/
E-MAIL   jcraddoc@tilc.com

SIGNATURE PRODUCT   **Cheesecake supreme**

NEWEST PRODUCT   Marvelous margarita cheesecake
ADDITIONAL PRODUCTS   Jubilations offers 40 flavors of cheesecakes in two sizes. All of our wonderful cheesecakes are made entirely from scratch. Only real butter, pure vanilla, and Philadelphia cream cheese are used.

COMMENTS   *This is truly outstanding cheesecake and is on the "must try" list.*

Knollwood Groves
8053 Lawrence Road
Boynton Beach, FL 33436-1699
PHONE (800) 222-9696; FAX (561) 737-6700

Lambs Farm

P.O. Box 520
Libertyville, IL 60048
PHONE (800) 52-LAMBS; FAX (847) 362-6319

La Vida Fina Bakery

P.O. Box 34280
Bethesda, MD 20827-0280
PHONE (800) 229-4916
WEB SITE   http://www.his.com/~vidafina/
E-MAIL   vidafina@his.com

SIGNATURE PRODUCT   **Molded cookies**

COMMENTS   *Very pretty molded cookies, plus they are delicious.*

Mack's Groves

1180 North Federal Highway
Pompano Beach, FL 33062
PHONE (800) 327-3525; FAX (954) 942-1463
WEB SITE   www.webpc.com/macks/
E-MAIL   macks@gate.net

Mary of Puddin Hill

4007 Interstate 30, P.O. Box 241
Greensville, TX 75403-0241
PHONE (800) 545-8889; FAX (903) 455-4522

SIGNATURE PRODUCT   **Pecan fruitcake**

NEWEST PRODUCT   Fruitcake cookies
ADDITIONAL PRODUCTS   Chocolates, nut brittles, sugar-free candies,
    pralines, pecan pie, butter rum cake, chocolate brandy cake, assort-
    ments of chocolate and fruit cake
COMMENTS   *It's fruit cake! And in every style you can imagine. Liked the nut-
    tiness of the fruit cake but thought there were too many cherries for my taste.*

Miss Grace Lemon Cake Co.

422 N. Canon Drive
Beverly Hills, CA 90210
PHONE (800) 367-2253; FAX (310) 668-2148

SIGNATURE PRODUCT *Lemon cake*

ADDITIONAL PRODUCTS Gracelets, cookies, chocolate truffle cake, orange cake, nuts and baskets

CATALOG INFO Pretty catalog with lots of enticing goodies.

COMMENTS *The lemon cake was perfect; exactly the way you would dream of a good lemon cake. It's on the "must try" list.*

Montreal Internet Deli & Catering

175 Poplar Road
Montreal, Quebec CANADA H9A 2A6
PHONE (514) 684-5321; FAX (514) 421-0534
WEB SITE http://www.vir.com/~can/bagel/
E-MAIL can@vir.com

Mrs. Beasley's Muffin & Gift Baskets

255 1/2 S. Beverly Drive
Beverly Hills, CA 90746
PHONE (800) MUFFIN1; FAX (310) 668-2148

Mrs. Peabody's Cookies

715 North University
Ann Arbor, MI 48104
PHONE (313) 761-2447; FAX (800) 761-2447

SIGNATURE PRODUCT *Heart-shaped cookies*

ADDITIONAL PRODUCTS Muffins (blueberry, chocolate chip, lemon, poppyseed, etc.), low-fat muffins and muffin tops, frozen yogurt, big cookie cakes, round or heart-shaped

COMMENTS *The cookies were all superior. My favorite was the white chip, heart-shaped cookie.*

Nordic House

3421 Telegraph Avenue
Oakland, CA 94609
PHONE (800) 854-6435; FAX (510) 653-1936
WEB SITE nordichouse.com
E-MAIL pia@nordichouse.com

O & H Danish Bakery

1841 Douglas Avenue
Racine, WI 53402
PHONE (800) 227-6665; FAX (414) 637-4215
WEB SITE www.bakery.com/oh.danish.kringle
E-MAIL ohdanish@wi.net

SIGNATURE PRODUCT **Danish Kringle (pecan flavored)**

NEWEST PRODUCT Kringle of the month club

Pane e Salute

61 Central Street
Woodstock, VT 05091
PHONE (802) 457-4882

SIGNATURE PRODUCT **Cantucci di Prato**

ADDITIONAL PRODUCTS Authentic almond biscotti, panettone (sweet
bread studded with citron, raisins and orange); pand'oro (bread baked
in a star-shaped mold); panforte (fruitcake); pizza civitavecchia (sweet
bread with ricotta and anise); and colomba pasquale (Easter bread)
COMMENTS *Absolutely wonderful, very unusual breads; a "must try."*

Priesters Pecan Co.

227 Old Fort Drive, P.O. Box 381
Fort Deposit, AL 36032
PHONE (800) 277-3226; FAX (334) 227-4294
WEB SITE www.priester.com

Rao's Bakery

2596 Calder
Beaumont, TX 77702
PHONE (800) 831-3098; FAX (409) 832-2011
WEB SITE www.setexas.com/raos
E-MAIL Raosbakery@aol.com

SIGNATURE PRODUCT **Mardi Gras King's Cake**

ADDITIONAL PRODUCTS We ship Mardi Gras King's Cake from
October through April. A King's Cake is the delicious rich coffee cake
served in Cajun country during Mardi Gras season

Rowena's

758 West 22nd Street
Norfolk, VA 23517
PHONE (800) 627-8699; FAX (804) 627-1505
WEB SITE pilotonline.com/Rowena's
E-MAIL Rowena's@aol.com

SIGNATURE PRODUCT **Almond poundcake/lemoncurd**

NEWEST PRODUCT Cranberry lemon torte
ADDITIONAL PRODUCTS Poundcakes: pecan praline, buttered rum,
chocolate turtle, double delicious chocolate, mocha, Amaretto, lemon,
coconut, and orange; also raspberry curd, cranberry nut conserve,
chocolate fudge sauce, praline sauce, barbecue sauce, curry sauce, hot
sauce, and mustard
CATALOG INFO Very comprehensive, nicely done
COMMENTS *Sent samples of almond poundcake, apricot ginger jam, lemon
curd, cranberry nut conserve and carrot jam. The poundcake was my favorite.*

Schroeder's Bakeries Inc.

212 Forest Avenue, P.O. Box 183
Buffalo, NY 14213-0183
PHONE (800) 850-7763; FAX (716) 885-0369
WEB SITE www.schroedersbakery.com
E-MAIL bakery@schroedersbakery.com

SIGNATURE PRODUCT   *Cakes-by-Mail Gifts*

NEWEST PRODUCT   Grandma's Country Muffin Basket
ADDITIONAL PRODUCTS   We offer bakery items such as cake, cake ornaments and supplies, gourmet coffees, spices and teas, and we have incorporated these items into several gift items.

The Sierra Shortbread Company

24040 Timber Ridge Drive
Auburn, CA 95602-8933
PHONE (800) 569-5982; FAX (916) 268-9142
WEB SITE   www.sierrashortbread.com
E-MAIL   sierrasb@inreach.com

SIGNATURE PRODUCT   *Grandma Pearlie's Shortbread Cookie*

ADDITIONAL PRODUCTS   We offer just this 100-year old family recipe for shortbread cookies baked in a small family bakery nestled in the Sierra Nevada foothills of California.
COMMENTS   *This is classic, wonderful shortbread; you can't go wrong with this.*

Stahmann's

P.O. Box 130
San Miguel, NM 88058-0130
PHONE (800) 654-6887; FAX (505) 526-7824
WEB SITE   www.stahmanns.com

Swiss Maid Bakery

104 E. Brainard Street
Harvard, IL 60033
PHONE (815) 943-4252; FAX (815) 943-4313
WEB SITE   www.bakery.com; E-MAIL   swissmaid@bakery.com

SIGNATURE PRODUCT   **Swiss Cinnamon Bears: One half pound cinnamon rolls oozing with korintje cinnamon and butter**

NEWEST PRODUCT   Pecan Sticky Bears
ADDITIONAL PRODUCTS   Streusel Crumb Cake; Almond Cluster Coffee Cake

Tasty Link Inc.
517 Lafayette Avenue
Wyckoff, NJ 07481
PHONE (201) 944-8021; FAX (201) 944-8183
WEB SITE http://www.websternet.com/tasty.html
E-MAIL sales@websternet.com

TECAPP srl
Lungotevere Flaminio 46
Rome Italy 196
PHONE ++396/321.51.15; FAX ++396/321.51.15
WEB SITE http://www.italiantidbits.com
E-MAIL e.romano@agora.stm.it

Tennessee T-Cakes

315 Tenth Avenue N, Suite 102
Nashville, TN 37203
PHONE (800) 883-9396; FAX (615) 256-3952
WEB SITE www.nashville.net/tntcakes
E-MAIL tntcakes@nashville.net

SIGNATURE PRODUCT **Tennessee T-cakes**

ADDITIONAL PRODUCTS The T-cakes are available in various sizes
COMMENTS *These are extraordinary, unlike anything else. This is a "must try" item. They also are beautifully packaged.*

Termini Bros.

1523 South 8th Street
Philadelphia, PA 19147
PHONE (800) 882-7650; FAX (215) 334-0535
WEB SITE www.termini.com

SIGNATURE PRODUCT **Authentic Italian, handmade cookies**

NEWEST PRODUCT Handmade Torrone tins of cookies
ADDITIONAL PRODUCTS Varieties of Italian cookies and candies handmade and using the best ingredients. And now Termini ships cannoli and some cakes, too

COMMENTS   *I love Italian cookies and these are excellent, the real thing. I have them on my "must try" list.*

Turf Cheesecake Co.
47 Halstead Avenue
Harrison, NY 10528
PHONE (800) 221-8873; FAX (914) 835-6793
WEB SITE   Turfcc.com
E-MAIL   Turfcc@aol.com

SIGNATURE PRODUCT   *NY Turf Cheesecake*

NEWEST PRODUCT   Old-fashioned apple cake
ADDITIONAL PRODUCTS   Assorted cheesecake flavors

Virginia Diner
P.O. Box 1030
Wakefield, VA 23888
PHONE (800) 868-6887; FAX (757) 899-2281
WEB SITE   www.vadiner.com
E-MAIL   vadiner@infi.net

Virtual Desserts
P.O. Box 12
Bayville, NY 11709
PHONE (516) 628-8297
WEB SITE   http://www.VirtualDesserts.com
E-MAIL   mzucaro@nassau.cv.net

SIGNATURE PRODUCT   *Cannoli*

NEWEST PRODUCT   Sfogliatella
ADDITIONAL PRODUCTS   Cheesecake

Wolferman's

One Muffin Lane, P.O. Box 15913
Lenexa, KS 66215
PHONE (800) 999-0169; FAX (800) 999-7548

SIGNATURE PRODUCT **Deluxe English muffins**

NEWEST PRODUCT Desserts
ADDITIONAL PRODUCTS Exquisite gifts of specialty foods including
English muffins, tea breads, scones, English muffin bread, crumpets,
hearth breads, brownies, dessert bars, and cinnamon rolls.
CATALOG INFO Nice catalog

Yasmin Gourmet Food

56 Pleasant Street
Greenville, RI 02828-1920
PHONE (401) 949-2121; FAX (401) 949-0991
WEB SITE hudson.idt.net/~brbina19/
E-MAIL bobbybina@hotmail.com

SIGNATURE PRODUCT **Baklava**

ADDITIONAL PRODUCTS Almond and pistachio baklava; seasoned
olive oils, vinegars, and chutney; marmalades; decorated fruit confections; dried fruit and nuts

CONDIMENTS & SAUCES

Mustards, oils, vinegars, jellies and jams, honey, hot sauces, butterscotch and chocolate sauce, syrups; also pestos and salsas.

3E Market
6753 Jones Mill Court, Suite A
Norcross, GA 30136
PHONE (800) 333-5548; FAX (800) 343-2652
WEB SITE http://www.3emarket.com
E-MAIL market@3e.com

American Spoon Foods, Inc.
1668 Clarion Avenue, P.O. Box 566
Petoskey, MI 49770
PHONE (800) 222-5886; FAX (616) 347-2512
WEB SITE www.spoon.com
E-MAIL information@spoon.com

Annie's Jellies & Jams
HC 37, Box 36
Valentine, NE 69201
PHONE (402) 376-2889; FAX (402) 376-1201
WEB SITE www.anniesjellies.com
E-MAIL annie@anniesjellies.com

SIGNATURE PRODUCT **Honey Jel**

NEWEST PRODUCT Very Berry Jam
ADDITIONAL PRODUCTS Chokeberry jelly, rose hip jelly, wild plum
jelly, wild grape jelly, Christmas jam, spiced peach jam, strawberry-
pineapple jam
COMMENTS *Annie is clearly a jelly and jam expert.*

Balducci's
11-02 Queens Plaza South
Long Island City, NY 11101
PHONE (800) 225-3822; FAX (718) 786-4125
WEB SITE www.balducci.com

Bandana Bandito

262 Hawthorn Commons, Suite 197
Vernon Hills, IL 60061
PHONE   (800) 880-5938;   FAX   (847) 680-0346
WEB SITE   http://www.bandito.com
E-MAIL   bandit@bandito.com

SIGNATURE PRODUCT   **Medium Salsa Ranchera**

NEWEST PRODUCT   Habanero Steak Sauce
ADDITIONAL PRODUCTS   Jalapeno mustard, medium BBQ sauce, hot
   BBQ sauce, medium bloody Mary mix, hot bloody Mary mix, hot red
   pepper sauce, black bean/corn salsa, chili con queso, hot green chili
   verde, hot red chili, rojo medium pecante sauce, hot pecante sauce
   and more
COMMENTS   *The Bandito's steak sauce was nice and spicy. I thought best for*
   hamburger or cube steak.

The Barbecue Source

8355 Riverbirch Drive
Roswell, GA 30076
PHONE (888) 252-7686;   FAX   (770) 552-0462
WEB SITE www.bbqsource.com
E-MAIL don@bbqsource

SIGNATURE PRODUCT   **Billy Bones BBQ Sauce**

NEWEST PRODUCT   Vann's Spices
ADDITIONAL PRODUCTS   Billy Bone's Dry Rub; BBQ Buddies Gift
   Pack; Texas Pete Hot Sauce and other BBQ paraphernalia
COMMENTS   *Good sauce! High in sugar content so watch the flames!*

Bates Nut Farm
15954 Woodsvalley Road
Valley Center, CA 92082
PHONE (760) 749-3333; FAX (760) 749-9499

Bear Kingdom Vineyard
P.O. Box 2316
Little Rock, AR 72203
PHONE (800) 781-1545; FAX (501) 888-1015
WEB SITE bbonline.com/~bbonline/vnd/bearkingdom/index.html
E-MAIL bearkingdom@juno.com

SIGNATURE PRODUCT Muscadine jelly

ADDITIONAL PRODUCTS Blackberry jam and jelly, cherry jelly, red
raspberry jam, strawberry jam and gift baskets
COMMENTS *Very nice muscadine jelly!*

Bewley Irish Imports
1130 Greenhill Road
West Chester, PA 19380
PHONE (610) 696-2682; FAX (610) 344-7618

Big Dave's
765 Quigley Road
Kelowna, British Columbia CANADA V1X 1A6
PHONE (250) 762-6867; FAX (250) 862-5828
WEB SITE www.geton.com/bdss
E-MAIL Dave_Abrahamse@bc.sympatico.ca

Birky's Cafe
205 South Main
Kouts, IN 46347
PHONE (219) 766-3851
WEB SITE birkycafe.com
E-MAIL jay@birkycafe.com

Bland Farms

P.O. Box 506-PG19
Glenndale, GA 30427
PHONE (800) 843-2542; FAX (912) 654-1330
WEB SITE www.blandfarms.com

The Blazing Chile Brothers

985 Quarry Street
Petaluma, CA 94954
PHONE (800) 473-9040; FAX (415) 332-1238
WEB SITE www.chilebros.com
E-MAIL Blazing@chilebros.com

SIGNATURE PRODUCT **Eclectic Mix of REALLY Hot Sauces/Salsas**

NEWEST PRODUCT Hussong's Cantina Sauces & Salsas (yeah the same Hussongs)

ADDITIONAL PRODUCTS We are adding 25 new outstanding products; but we have limited our inventory to about 125 of the very best sauces, salsas, BBQs, jerks, marinades and munchies. While the heat is definitely there, flavor is the highest priority.

Blood's Hammock Groves

4600 Linton Boulevard
Delray Beach, FL 33445
PHONE (800) 255-5188; FAX (561) 498-0285
WEB SITE www.bhgcitrus.com
E-MAIL blood's@bhgcitrus.com

Bluebonnet Gourmet

P.O. Box 132145
Tyler, TX 75712-2145
PHONE (800) 657-1895; FAX (903) 509-8000
WEB SITE www.bluebonnetgourmet.com
E-MAIL blubonet@gower.net

SIGNATURE PRODUCT **Texas-style condiments**

ADDITIONAL PRODUCTS Sweet jalapeno relish, black bean salsa, salsa

caliente, and jalapeno pepper jelly; mixed cases available
COMMENTS   *Loved that sweet jalapeno relish, perfect blend of sweet and hot!*

▓ Boehms Chocolates
1101 Supermall Way #1332
Auburn, WA 98001
PHONE   (206) 735-1994;   FAX   (206) 735-1911
WEB SITE   www.forsuccess.com/chocolate/boehms
E-MAIL   boehms@wolfenet.com

Boo-Daddy's Chile Pepper Company

P.O. Box 6245
North Augusta, SC 29861-6245
PHONE (800) 436-6794; FAX (706) 790-9898
WEB SITE   www.augusta.net/boo_daddy's/
E-MAIL   Rkeller@augusta.net

SIGNATURE PRODUCT   **Dave's Insanity Hot Sauce**

NEWEST PRODUCT   Spontaneous Combustion
ADDITIONAL PRODUCTS   Gourmet chile pepper hot sauces, salsas,
    and cajun mixes; also Ass Kickin' cornbread, Panola jalapeno jelly
    beans, gift baskets and more
COMMENTS   *The rice jambalaya readi-mix was terrific; nice for this New
    Englander to have a good source for jambalaya.*

▓ The British Gourmet
45 Wall Street
Madison, CT 06443
PHONE (800) 842-6674;   FAX (203) 245-3477
WEB SITE   www.thebritishshoppe.com
E-MAIL   gourmet@thebritisheshoppe.com

C.S. Steen Syrup Mill Inc.

119 North Main Street, P.O. Box 339
Abbeville, LA 70511-0339
PHONE (800) 725-1654; FAX (318) 893-2478
WEB SITE   WWW.STEENSYRUP.COM

E-MAIL   Steens@iamerica.net

SIGNATURE PRODUCT   *Steen's 100% Pure Cane Syrup*

NEWEST PRODUCT   Steen's Pure Cane Vinegar

ADDITIONAL PRODUCTS   Steen's syrup mill also produces the only pure cane molasses in the country and a cane/corn syrup blend known as "Southern Made."

COMMENTS   *Pure cane syrup is difficult to get in a supermarket and I like to use it when making sorbets instead of refined, granulated sugar. It really adds great flavor.*

Cafe Beaujolais Bakery
961 Ukiah Street, P.O. Box 730
Mendocino, CA 95460
PHONE (800) 930-0443; FAX (707) 937-3656
WEB SITE   www.cafebeaujolais.com
E-MAIL   cafebeau@men.org

Calef's Country Store
Route 9, P.O. Box 57
Barrington, NH 03825
PHONE (603) 664-2231; FAX (603) 664-5857
WEB SITE   www.wertzcandy.com
E-MAIL   wertz@nbn.net

Callaway Gardens
P.O. Box 2000
Pine Mountain, GA 31822-2000
PHONE (800) 280-7524; FAX (706) 663-5058

Caviar Delight & Gifts Company
33020 10th Avenue, SW Suite P302
Federal Way, WA 98023
PHONE (800) 572-6180 access code 50; FAX (253) 835-0468
WEB SITE   www.caviargift.com
E-MAIL   sales@caviargift.com

Chachka

905 River Road
Erwinna, PA 18920
PHONE (610) 294-9763
WEB SITE http://www.arsdata.com/chachka
E-MAIL chachka@epix.net

SIGNATURE PRODUCT **Homemade jams, relishes and chutneys**

NEWEST PRODUCT Garlic Honey
ADDITIONAL PRODUCTS Our homemade jams, relishes and chutneys
have national recognition.

Chili Bob Products Inc.

P.O. Box 219
Oak Harbor, OH 43449
PHONE (419) 732-8281; FAX (417) 732-3780
WEB SITE www.chilibob.com; E-MAIL email@chilibobb.com

SIGNATURE PRODUCT **Chili Bob's Mean Mother Chili Mix**

NEWEST PRODUCT "Ohio's Best!" Salsa
ADDITIONAL PRODUCTS Onion lovers, pepper lovers & garlic lovers
gourmet seasonings: Island Fever Powdered Hot Sauce (the World's
only!); Coming Soon: Mean Mother Wing Sauce, Mean Mother
Mustard, Ben's Bitchin' BBQ Baste, Chili Dick's Wicked Weinnie
Sauce and more
COMMENTS *Ohio's Best! salsa was nice and spicy, and in addition to being
a good salsa I added it to my spaghetti sauce and it was terrific.*

Cibolo Junction Food & Spice Company Inc.

3013 Aztec Road NE
Albuquerque, NM 87107
PHONE (800) 683-9628; FAX (505) 888-1972
WEB SITE www.cibolojunction.com
E-MAIL info@cibolojunction.com

SIGNATURE PRODUCT **Green Chile Stew & Red Chile Strawberry
Preserve**

NEWEST PRODUCT   Mango Papaya Salsa with Tomatillo

ADDITIONAL PRODUCTS   Bowl O' Red Chili (mild & hot); Sopa Festival Soup; Chili Blanco Soup; Feast Day Posole Stew; Homestead Sausage Bread; Indian Blue Cornbread; Preserves: Red Chile, Green Chile, Jalapeno Pepper, Green Chile Pineapple, Habanero Peach and more

COMMENTS   *The mango papaya salsa was wild! Think I'll try it atop chicken breasts next.*

Classic Kansas City Barbeque Sauces

6105 Manning
Raytown, MO 64133
PHONE (816) 356-9278
WEB SITE http://worldmall.com/bbq/bbq.htm
E-MAIL bbq@worldmall.com

SIGNATURE PRODUCT   **Kansas City Restaurant BBQ Sauces**

NEWEST PRODUCT   BBQ Video

ADDITIONAL PRODUCTS   KC Restaurant BBQ sauces and rubs; Kansas City related BBQ books, BBQ video, BBQ flavored toasted almonds

Coppola Enterprise

6102 Mockingbird Lane, Suite 251
Dallas, TX 75214
FAX (972) 270-2700
E-MAIL hco739@airmail.net

SIGNATURE PRODUCT   **Howlin' Hot Sauce**

Cosmopolitan Foods

138 Essex Avenue
Glen Ridge, NJ 07042
PHONE (201) 680-4560
WEB SITE www.hotchilisauce.com
E-MAIL hotchilisauce@juno.com

▦ Country Sliced Ham
1321 Guerneville Road
Santa Rosa, CA 95401
PHONE (707) 523-1655
WEB SITE http://netmar.com/~hamorder
E-MAIL custom@sonic.net

▦ Country Store
R.D. #2, Box P31
Pennsdale, PA 17756
PHONE (800) 313-HAMS; FAX (717) 546-8626
WEB SITE www.sunlink.net/%7Ectrystre
E-MAIL ctrystre@earth.sunlink.net

Coyote Moon

▐▌

1709 South Braddick Avenue
Pittsburgh, PA 15218
PHONE (412) 594-4830; FAX (412) 242-8710
WEB SITE spicyhot.com/coyotemoon/
E-MAIL coyote@spicyhot.com

SIGNATURE PRODUCT **Hot sauce and salsas, Fiery foods**

NEWEST PRODUCT Artichoke tepenade
ADDITIONAL PRODUCTS Specializing in mid-range, spicy products
from the East coast, including hot sauces, salsas, pretzels, peanuts,
habanero, chili mixes, stuffed olives, dilli beans, mustards, pepper
sauces, spicy snacks, barbecue and wing sauces, and gift baskets.
COMMENTS *The Seductive Dessert Salsa (chocolate-raspberries diablo) is
very surprising. It sounds like a hot sauce that's chocolate which wouldn't
be good, but it's really quite tasty.*

▦ Dakin Farm
Route 7, RR1, Box 1775
Ferrisburg, VT 05456
PHONE (800) 993-2546; FAX (802) 425-2765
WEB SITE www.dakinfarm.com
E-MAIL dakin@vbimail.champlain.edu

Daniel Weaver Company
15th Avenue & Weavertown Road, P.O. Box 525
Lebanon, PA 17042
PHONE (800) WEAVERS; FAX (717) 274-6103

Dave's Gourmet Inc.
1255 Montgomery Avenue
San Bruno, CA 94066
PHONE (800) 758-0372; FAX (415) 794-0340
WEB SITE davesgourmet.com
E-MAIL insanity@davesgourmet.com

SIGNATURE PRODUCT **Insanity Sauce**

NEWEST PRODUCT Bonsal & Lloyd Kalamata & Garlic Mayonnaise
ADDITIONAL PRODUCTS Total Insanity Sauce, Hurtin' Habanero
Sauce, Insanity Salsa, Insanity Snax, Udderly Insane Cheese, Insanity
Sausage, Demented Dills, Mad Mushrooms plus shirts, hats, baskets,
cooking sauces, salad dressings, etc.

Delftree Mushrooms
234 Union Street
North Adams, MA 02147
PHONE (800) 243-3742; FAX (413) 664-4908

Desert Rose Foods
P.O. Box 5391
Tucson, AZ 85703
PHONE (800) 937-2572; FAX (520) 620-0406

SIGNATURE PRODUCT **Salsa**

ADDITIONAL PRODUCTS Several different types of salsa; plus mustards, catsup, hot sauce, marinated peppers, tortilla chips, candy and
gift packs
COMMENTS *There really was something special about this salsa. It had plen-
ty of flavor and was spicy hot but not to the point where the taste got lost. I
think it should be on the "must try" list.*

DiBruno Bros. House of Cheese
930 South 9th Street
Philadelphia, PA 19147
PHONE (888) 322-4337; FAX (215) 922-2080
WEB SITE http://www.dibruno.com
E-MAIL dibruno@gim.net

Dixie Chili
Newport, KY 41071
PHONE (606) 291-5337 & (606) 291-5337; FAX (606) 291-5547
WEB SITE www.dixiechili.com; E-MAIL dixiechili@fuse.net

Farmacopia
21900 Summit Road
Los Gatos, CA 95030
PHONE (888) 353-5577; FAX (408) 353-2875
WEB SITE www.farmacopia.com
E-MAIL sbfm@farmacopia.com

Ferris Valley Groves
P.O. Box 530567
Harlingen, TX 78553-0567
PHONE (800) 748-7182; FAX (210) 412-6148
E-MAIL sarah@valleygroves.com

Flying Fajitas
13710 Chittim Oak
San Antonio, TX 78232
PHONE (800) 290-3411
WEB SITE www.fajitas.com
E-MAIL Flyingfajitas@stic.net

Flying Noodle
1 Arrowhead Road
Duxbury, MA 02332
PHONE (800) 566-0599; FAX (617) 934-1527
WEB SITE www.flyingnoodle.com
E-MAIL bigparmesan@flyingnoodle.com

The Garlic Survival Company
1094-A1 Revere Avenue
San Francisco, CA 94124
PHONE (800) 3GARLIC; FAX (415) 822-6224

SIGNATURE PRODUCT *Garlic pesto*

ADDITIONAL PRODUCTS Garlic salsa, garlic BBQ sauce, crushed garlic, garlic braids, garlic cocktail sauce, garlic mustard, garlic pasta sauce, garlic salt and other garlic seasonings. Plus garlic accessories and kits

Gazin's
2910 Toulouse Street, P.O. Box 19221
New Orleans, LA 70119-0221
PHONE (800) 262-6410; FAX (504) 827-5319

Get Sauced!
115 Elizabeth Drive, P.O. Box 426
Manteo, NC 27954
PHONE (800) 948-0224; FAX (919) 473-6879
WEB SITE www.getsauced.com; E-MAIL getsauced@interpath.com

SIGNATURE PRODUCT *Sauces*

NEWEST PRODUCT Melina's cold-pressed extra virgin olive oil & balsamic vinegar
ADDITIONAL PRODUCTS Katch This Ketchup, Dr. Monty's Love Potion, Georgia Peach Mix, Gilly's Hot Vanilla, Hatteras Hoppin' John Dried Soup Mix, Nick's Greek Salad Dressing, Prairie Fire Salsas, Chunky Olive Pesto Pasta Sauce, Dave's Insanity Sauce, Golden Garlic Pate and more!
COMMENTS *The Swamp Sauce was GREAT!*

Gifts from the Illinois Amish Country
138 S. Vine
Arthur, IL 61911
PHONE (800) 879-2494; FAX (217) 543-2898
WEB SITE www.IllinoisAmishCountry.com/WLPantry/gifthome.htm
E-MAIL AmishCM@net66.com

The Gourmet Trading Company
1071 Avenida Acaso
Camarillo, CA 93012
PHONE (800) 888-3484; FAX (805) 389-4790
WEB SITE www.gourmettrader.com
E-MAIL trader@gourmettrader.com

Grandma's Gourmet
P.O. Box 137
Black Creek, British Columbia CANADA V9N 1K8
PHONE (250) 337-8127; FAX (250) 337-8261

SIGNATURE PRODUCT **Nippy Basting Sauce**

ADDITIONAL PRODUCTS Lemon Rosemary Jelly
COMMENTS *The lemon rosemary jelly was very nice on salmon, very delicate enhancement of flavor.*

Granny's Secret Foods
P.O. Box 515
Pilomath, OR 97370
PHONE (800) 654-3663
WEB SITE http://pioneer net/~grannys/sauce.htm
E-MAIL grannys@pioneer.net

SIGNATURE PRODUCT *Granny's Secret Barbeque Sauce*

ADDITIONAL PRODUCTS Granny's secret barbecue sauce is terrific, I can see why Granny keeps the recipe a secret. And it would be difficult to analyze what makes it so special, definitely worth buying

Great Food Online
2030 1st Avenue, 3rd Floor
Seattle, WA 98121
PHONE (800) 841-5984; FAX (206) 443-3314
WEB SITE http://www.greatfood.com
E-MAIL proprietor@greatfood.com

The Great Southern Sauce Company

5705 Kavanaugh
Little Rock, AR 72207
PHONE (800) 437-2823; FAX (501) 663-0956
WEB SITE   www.greatsauce.com

SIGNATURE PRODUCT   *Sauces*

ADDITIONAL PRODUCTS   Over 1,500 different products: sauces; jerk, barbecue, marinades; also salsas, rubs and gift boxes

Green Briar Jam Kitchen

6 Discovery Hill Road
East Sandwich, MA 02537
PHONE (508) 888-6870; FAX (508) 888-1919
WEB SITE   www.capecod.net/tburgess
E-MAIL   tburgess@capecod.net

SIGNATURE PRODUCT   *Sun-cooked fruit toppings*

NEWEST PRODUCT   Cape Cod salsa
ADDITIONAL PRODUCTS   Jams, jellies, pickles, relishes, marmalades, and cranberry products

Green Mountain Sugar House

Box 82, Route 100N
Ludlow, VT 05149
PHONE (800) 643-9338; FAX (802) 228-2298
E-MAIL   gmsh@ludl.tds.net

SIGNATURE PRODUCT   *Maple syrup*

ADDITIONAL PRODUCTS   Maple syrup in many sizes and attractive containers, maple cream and candy; Vermont cheese, mincemeat pies, bacon, Green Mountain coffee, Vermont Breakfast pancakes, other Vermont products; also a variety of gift packages
COMMENTS   *The maple candy is terrific! And should mean so is the syrup.*

Heaton Pecan Farm
309 Sunrise Boulevard
Clanton, AL 35045
PHONE (800) 446-3531; FAX (205) 755-8677

The Homestead Sugar House

11393 Homestead Road
Beulah, MI 49617
PHONE (616) 882-7712

SIGNATURE PRODUCT **Maple products**

ADDITIONAL PRODUCTS   Maple syrup, sugar, candies, chocolates,
hand-dipped cherries, chocolate and peanut butter fudge, fruit syrups,
dietetic candies, honey and more
COMMENTS   *Their fruit syrups are wonderful, very, very flavorful. I particularly liked the marionberry syrup.*

Hosgood's Company
P.O. Box 1265
Strafford, TX 77497-1265
PHONE (800) 4-GARLIC
WEB SITE   www.4garlic.com

Hot Pursuits
P.O. Box 176
North Gower, Ontario CANADA K0A 2T0
PHONE (613) 489-0744
WEB SITE   http://www.hotpursuits.com
E-MAIL   kdpepper@hotpursuits.com

SIGNATURE PRODUCT **Hot Sauce**

NEWEST PRODUCT   14 new sauces
ADDITIONAL PRODUCTS   Hot and Spicy cookbooks

Hot's Desire

11267 Price Court
Riverside, CA 92503
PHONE (800) 381-4687
WEB SITE http:/www.machines.com/hotsdesr
E-MAIL hotsdesr@deltanet.com

SIGNATURE PRODUCT *Hot Sauces*

NEWEST PRODUCT Pepper dated plates
ADDITIONAL PRODUCTS Salsas, books, barbecue sauces, mustards all
with peppers

The Hot Shop

P.O. Box 7917
North Augusta, SC 29861-7917
PHONE (888) 850-HOTT; FAX (803) 202-0395
WEB SITE www.hotstuff4u.com
E-MAIL rjenkins@gabn.net

SIGNATURE PRODUCT *Hot sauces*

ADDITIONAL PRODUCTS Hot salsas and more

House Of Fire

1108 Spruce Street
Boulder, CO 80302
PHONE (800) 717-5787; FAX (303) 447-8685
WEB SITE www.houseoffire.com
E-MAIL info@houseoffire.com

SIGNATURE PRODUCT *Over 500 Hot & Spicy Foods From Around
The World. Including over 200 hot sauces!*

NEWEST PRODUCT New products on a regular basis
ADDITIONAL PRODUCTS Products include: Hot Sauce, salsa, BBQ
sauces, mustards, oils, vinegars, spices, Thai and Indonesian marinades and sauces, Indian currys, wing sauces, jams & jellys, peanut
butter, jerk sauce, fajita marinades, candies, nuts, pickled chiles

The Island Gourmet Shop

c/o M & W of Jax Inc.
2727-6 Clydo Road
Jacksonville, FL 32207
PHONE (800) 335-7880; FAX (904) 730-0494
WEB SITE http://www.islandgourmet.com
E-MAIL brhoden@islandgourmet.com

SIGNATURE PRODUCT *Batten Island Gourmet Sauce*

Jasmine & Bread

RR #2, Box 256
South Royalton, VT 05068
PHONE (802) 763-7115

SIGNATURE PRODUCT *Sweet lightning horseradish jelly*

NEWEST PRODUCT Champagne jelly and mango jazz
ADDITIONAL PRODUCTS Marinades, sauces, jellies, mustards, catsup
COMMENTS *I especially liked their Caribbean Heat sauce; hot but not too, very good in soup.*

K.E. Farm

317 Leadmine Road, P.O. Box 616
Sturbridge, MA 01566
PHONE (508) 347-9323
WEB SITE http://www.choicemall.com./maplesyrup
E-MAIL http://www.kefarm@hey.net

SIGNATURE PRODUCT *Maple syrup*

COMMENTS *It's maple syrup!*

Kalmar Enterprises Inc.

P.O. Box 3677
Portland, ME 04104
PHONE (207) 642-2813; FAX (207) 642-2813
WEB SITE http://www.pivot.net/~kalmaine

E-MAIL   kalmaine@pivot.net

SIGNATURE PRODUCT   *Mustards*

NEWEST PRODUCT   Sauces
ADDITIONAL PRODUCTS   Marinated garlic, jams & jellies, pepper jellies, salad dressings, Maine maple syrup and Maine honey

KIBCO

P.O. Box 565
Belgrade Lakes, ME 04918
PHONE (207) 495-7749; FAX   Call first
WEB SITE   malls.com/awesome/kibco.html
E-MAIL   kibco@gwi.net

SIGNATURE PRODUCT   *Piquant Sauce*

NEWEST PRODUCT   Piquant Smokey Hot Sauce
ADDITIONAL PRODUCTS   Piquant Tangy, Piquant Tangy Hot, Piquant Smokey
COMMENTS   *This is fantastic, really better in my mind than plain ol' barbecue sauce.*

Knollwood Groves
8053 Lawrence Road
Boynton Beach, FL 33436-1699
PHONE   (800) 222-9696;   FAX   (561) 737-6700

Krema Nut Company
1000 W. Goodale Boulevard
Columbus, OH 43212
PHONE (614) 299-4131; FAX (614) 299-1636
WEB SITE   www.krema.com
E-MAIL   nuts@krema.com

Lambs Farm
P.O. Box 520
Libertyville, IL 60048
PHONE (800) 52-LAMBS; FAX (847) 362-6319

Los Chileros de Nuevo Mexico
P.O. Box 6215
Sante Fe, NM 87502
PHONE (505) 471-6967; FAX (505) 473-7306
WEB SITE www.hotchilepepper.com/ordering.htm

Louisiana French Market Online
4614 Tupello Street
Baton Rouge, LA 70808
PHONE (504) 928-1428; FAX 504-774-4085
WEB SITE http://www.louisianafrenchmarket.com
E-MAIL service@louisianafrenchmarket.com

Mack's Groves
1180 North Federal Highway
Pompano Beach, FL 33062
PHONE (800) 327-3525; FAX (954) 942-1463
WEB SITE www.webpc.com/macks/; E-MAIL macks@gate.net

Magic Seasonings
New Orleans, LA 70123
PHONE (800) 457-2857; FAX (501) 731-3579
WEB SITE www.chefpaul.com; E-MAIL info@chefpaul.com

Maison Louisianne Creole Products

2212 19th Street
San Francisco, CA 94107
PHONE (415) 285-7731; FAX (415) 285-7731
WEB SITE www.shutmymouth.com
E-MAIL creole@shutmymouth.com

SIGNATURE PRODUCT **Creole mustard**

NEWEST PRODUCT Creole "Shut My Mouth" marinade
ADDITIONAL PRODUCTS Creole "Shut My Mouth" pepper sauce, creole "Shut My Mouth" spices
COMMENTS *The mustard was awesome. As Lawrence Ames (a.k.a. president of "Shut My Mouth") says, "spicy, not hot, the true Creole flavor."*

Manganaro Foods
488 Ninth Avenue
New York, NY 10018
PHONE (800) 4-SALAMI; FAX (212) 239-8355

Maurice's Gourmet Barbeque
1600 Charleston Highway, P.O. Box 6847
West Columbia, SC 29171
PHONE (803) 791-5887; FAX (803) 791-8707
WEB SITE http://www.mauricesbbq.com
E-MAIL maurices@netside.com

SIGNATURE PRODUCT *Original Carolina Gold BBQ sauce*

NEWEST PRODUCT BBQ frozen dinner
ADDITIONAL PRODUCTS Five flavors of Sauce: Original, Honey
  Recipe, Spicy, Hickory and our new all-purpose table sauce. Frozen
  all-ham barbeque; frozen all-ham barbeque dinners includes all-ham
  BBQ, baked beans, white fluffy rice and hash
COMMENTS *Maurice's is really great BBQ sauce!*

Mendocino Mustard
1260 North Main Street
Fort Bragg, CA 95437
PHONE (800) 964-2270; FAX (707) 964-0525

SIGNATURE PRODUCT *Hot & sweet mustard*

ADDITIONAL PRODUCTS Seeds & Suds (made with Red Seal Ale),
  mustards in a variety of sizes

Midwest Pepper Trading Company
3 Swannanoa Drive
Rochester, IL 62563
PHONE (217) 498-9233; FAX (217) 498-9233
WEB SITE www.midwestpepper.com
E-MAIL mcdon@midwestpepper.com

SIGNATURE PRODUCT   *World's Best Hot Sauces and Salsas*

NEWEST PRODUCT   1997 Fiery Foods Show Winners
ADDITIONAL PRODUCTS   The Best of the Best hot sauces, salsas and other pepper-related products.

Miguel's Stowe Away

RR3, Box 2086
Waterbury, VT 05676
PHONE (800) 448-6517; FAX (802) 244-7804
E-MAIL   miguels@together.net

SIGNATURE PRODUCT   *Blue & white tortilla chips and salsa*

NEWEST PRODUCT   Baked white & blue corn tortilla chips (low-fat)
ADDITIONAL PRODUCTS   Mild, medium, hot roasted garlic and green chile salsas, no-salt white or blue corn tortilla chips, white cheddar cheese flavor, salsa-flavored chips, smoked jalapeno fajita sauce
COMMENTS   *The blue corn tortilla chips were exceptional, I've changed my brand to Miguel's now.*

Mixon Fruit Farms Inc.

2712 26th Avenue E
Bradenton, FL 34208
PHONE (800) 608-2525; FAX (941) 748-1085
WEB SITE   www.mixon.com
E-MAIL   Info@mixon.com

Mo Hotta — Mo Betta

P. O. Box 4136
San Luis Obispo, CA 93401
PHONE (800) 462-3220; FAX (800) 618-4454
WEB SITE   mohotta.com
E-MAIL   mohotta@mohotta.com

SIGNATURE PRODUCT   *Hot & spicy food products*

NEWEST PRODUCT   Our own line of hot sauces
CATALOG INFO   Very complete

✳ MontBlanc Gourmet Hot Cocoa
425 South Cherry, Suite 630
Denver, CO 80222
PHONE (800) 877-3811; FAX (303) 399-1616
WEB SITE www.montblancgourmet.com
E-MAIL mtblanc@montblancgourmet.com

New Generation Food Products
7799 S.W. Cirrus Drive
Beaverton, OR 97008
PHONE (800) 790-6860; FAX (503) 644-6752
WEB SITE www.teleport.com~saucg/
E-MAIL sauce@teleport.com

SIGNATURE PRODUCT **Hollandaise, bearnaise sauce**

NEWEST PRODUCT Jalapeno sauce
ADDITIONAL PRODUCTS Dill hollandaise
COMMENTS *If you're too busy to make your own hollandaise (or fear yet another failure), these sauces are very good substitutes for homemade.*

✳ Nordic House
3421 Telegraph Avenue
Oakland, CA 94609
PHONE (800) 854-6435; FAX (510) 653-1936
WEB SITE nordichouse.com
E-MAIL pia@nordichouse.com

Off The Deep End
712 East Street
Frederick, MD 21701
PHONE (800) 248-045; FAX (301) 698-0375
WEB SITE http://www.offthedeepend.com
E-MAIL chilimon@offthedeepend.com

SIGNATURE PRODUCT **We have 125+ hot sauces and hot food products**

ADDITIONAL PRODUCTS Hot sauces, salsas, hot snacks, oils, vinegars and chile related gifts

▦ **Oinkers**
1500 E. 7th
Atlantic, IA 50022
PHONE (712) 243-3606; FAX (712) 243-5688
WEB SITE   www.neyins.net.\showcaseoinkers

▦ **Only Gourmet**
P.O. Box 2214
Orinda, CA 94563
PHONE (888) 413-6637; FAX (510) 531-4981
WEB SITE   http://www.onlygourmet.com
E-MAIL   alank@onlygourmet.com

Oregon Hill Farms

32861 Pittsburg Road
St. Helens, OR 97051
PHONE (800) 243-4541; FAX (503) 397-2791

SIGNATURE PRODUCT   *Gourmet fruit products*

NEWEST PRODUCT   Naturally sweetened fruit spreads; marionberry,
   raspberry, blueberry
ADDITIONAL PRODUCTS   Fruit jams, syrups, jellies, spreads
COMMENTS   *I really liked their pumpkin butter.*

▦ **The Oriental Pantry**
423 Great Road
Acton, MA 01720
PHONE (800) 828-0368; FAX (617) 275-4506
WEB SITE   www.orientalpantry.com
E-MAIL   oriental@orientalpantry.com

Pan Handler Products

1799 Mountain Road
Stowe, VT 05672
PHONE (800) 338-5354; FAX (802) 253-7139
E-MAIL   vtharvest@aol.com

SIGNATURE PRODUCT *Apple rum walnut conserve*

NEWEST PRODUCT Smokin' garlic tomato spread
ADDITIONAL PRODUCTS Jellies, jams, conserves, and mustards
COMMENTS *Especially liked the tomato chutney!*

Panola Pepper Corp.
Route 2, Box 148
Lake Providence, LA 71254
PHONE (800) 256-3013; FAX (318) 559-3003
WEB SITE www.southernnet.com/panola_peppers

SIGNATURE PRODUCT **Pepper sauces**

NEWEST PRODUCT Jalapeno mustard
ADDITIONAL PRODUCTS Hot sauces, jalapeno stuffed olives, peppers, readi-mixes and seasonings. Meals: red beans & rice, jambalaya, and gumbo
COMMENTS *The jalapeno mustard was terrific, particularly served on a hot dog!*

Pasta Concerto
1240 E. Lombard Street, Suite 102
Thousand Oaks, CA 91360
PHONE (805) 374-7152; FAX (805) 496-5598
WEB SITE pastaconcerto.com
E-MAIL pastaconcerto@lab-net.com

SIGNATURE PRODUCT **22 unique pasta sauces**

NEWEST PRODUCT Yellow sundried tomato and goat cheese pesto

Pasta Just For You By Sue
111 West Main
West Dundee, IL 60118
PHONE (800) PASTA-US; FAX (847) 836-1014

Pepper Island Beach

P.O. Box 484
Lawrence, PA 15055
PHONE (412) 746-2401; FAX (412) 746-1679
WEB SITE www.pepperisland.com
E-MAIL peppers@nauticom.net

SIGNATURE PRODUCT **Hot sauces**

ADDITIONAL PRODUCTS Habanero Hurricane, Crocodile Soup,
Pirates Attack, St. Blaze's Cure
COMMENTS *Habanero Hurricane is a little fruity kind of hot
sauce . . . hot and nice!*

Pezzini Farms

460 Nashua Road, P.O. Box 1276
Castroville, CA 95012
PHONE (800) 347-6118; FAX (408) 757-4476
WEB SITE www.pezzinifarms.com
E-MAIL artichoke@pezzinifarms.com

The Pikled Garlik

P.O. Box 846
Pacific Grove, CA 93950
PHONE (800) 775-9788; FAX (408) 393-1709

Piquant Pepper

P.O. Box 20196
Wichita, KS 67208-1196
PHONE (800) 931-7474; FAX (316) 685-9144
WEB SITE www.shipnizzy.com
E-MAIL piquant@dtc.net

SIGNATURE PRODUCT **Awesome selection of hot stuff**

NEWEST PRODUCT Sug, Black Dog Salsa, FakoFire
ADDITIONAL PRODUCTS Over 364 quality products
CATALOG INFO Very comprehensive catalog
COMMENTS *Loved that Sug!*

Pit Boss Enterprises

2364 West Hardies Road
Gibsonia, PA 15044-8328
PHONE (412) 444-6253; FAX (412) 444-6273
WEB SITE   www.pitbossbbq.com
E-MAIL   pitboss@pitbossbbq.com

SIGNATURE PRODUCT   **Smokestack Lightning Barbecue Sauce**

COMMENTS   *The Pit Boss Smokestack barbecue sauce was justn great; a zippy, kind of spicy sauce.*

PMS Foods Inc.

2701 East 11th Avenue, P.O. Box 1099
Hutchinson, KS 67504-1099
PHONE (800) 835-5006; FAX (316) 663-7195
WEB SITE   http://www.bbqsauce.com
E-MAIL   sales@pmsfoods.com

SIGNATURE PRODUCT   **Curley's Famous Hickory Barbecue Sauce**

NEWEST PRODUCT   Curley's Honey Dijon Barbecue Sauce
ADDITIONAL PRODUCTS   We also have the following flavors available: mesquite, smoky, hot & spicy
COMMENTS   *Curley has great barbecue sauce!*

POP 'N STUFF INC.

Broadway at the Beach, 1303 Celebrity Circle 125
Myrtle Beach, SC 29577
PHONE (800) 735-5440; FAX (803) 946-6813
WEB SITE   http://sccoast.net/popn/popnstuf/home.htm:
E-MAIL   popn@sccoast.net

Pueblo Harvest Foods

San Juan Agriculture Cooperative, P.O. Box 1188
San Juan Pueblo, NM 87566
PHONE (888) 511-1120; FAX (505) 747-3148
WEB SITE   www.puebloharvest.com
E-MAIL   puebloharv@aol.com

Putnam Family Farm

RR 2, Box 2805
Cambridge, VT 05444
PHONE (802) 644-2267; FAX (802) 644-6506
WEB SITE   www.sover.net/~bputnam/index.htm
E-MAIL   bputnam@sover.net

SIGNATURE PRODUCT   Maple syrup

ADDITIONAL PRODUCTS   The Putnam Family has been producing
maple syrup since 1863, and it's their only mail-order product.
COMMENTS   *It is very nice maple syrup.*

Rainforest Honey Co.

314 Colby Drive
Dartmouth, Nova Scotia CANADA B2V 2B6
PHONE (902) 462-0680; FAX (902) 462-0680
WEB SITE   http://www.isisnet.com/MAX/ads/honey.html
E-MAIL   rainforesthoneyco@ns.sympatico.ca

SIGNATURE PRODUCT   **Tasmanian Leatherwood honey**

NEWEST PRODUCT   Dr. Stuart's Botanical and Herbal Teas
ADDITIONAL PRODUCTS   Tasmanian Meadow honey; Tropical
Rainforest honey; Tasmanian Leatherwood & Ginger; Tasmanian
Leatherwood & Apricot; Tasmanian Leatherwood & Apple
COMMENTS   *The Tasmanian Leatherwood honey is absolutely extraordinary!*
Worth getting just for the aroma; definitely on the "must try" list.

R.L. Pearson & Sons

P.O. Box 1892
Winter Haven, FL 33883-1892
PHONE (888) 438-3565
WEB SITE   www.juiceking.com
E-MAIL   info@juiceking.com

Red River of Death

28-27 48 Street
Astoria, NY 11103
PHONE (718) 721-5475
WEB SITE http://www.pcompute.com/ra/redriver.htm
E-MAIL SauceBoss1@aol.com

SIGNATURE PRODUCT **Red River of Death Hot Salsa**

NEWEST PRODUCT Soho(t) Salsa
COMMENTS *This was absolutely fantastic salsa. Hot, but not as death defying hot as the name might indicate, and with a nice lemon-y taste. It's on my "must try" list.*

Robert's Orchard

RR2, Box 2165
Belfast, ME 04915
PHONE (800) 251-7915

SIGNATURE PRODUCT **Honey spreads**

NEWEST PRODUCT Seven flavors of spreads
ADDITIONAL PRODUCTS Wild Maine blueberry, cinnamon, and other flavors plus butter/margarine substitute

Rossi Pasta Factory Inc.

114 Greene Street, P.O. Box 759
Marietta, OH 45750
PHONE (800) 227-6774; FAX (614) 373-5310
WEB SITE www.civic.net/webmarket/ then select Rossi Pasta
E-MAIL 102121.2140@compuserve.com

Rowena's

758 West 22nd Street
Norfolk, VA 23517
PHONE (800) 627-8699; FAX (804) 627-1505
WEB SITE pilotonline.com/Rowena's
E-MAIL Rowena's@aol.com

Sam McGees Hot Gourmet

8995 Finucane
Hayden, ID 83835
PHONE (208) 762-2627
WEB SITE http://sammcgees.com
E-MAIL troxel@nidlink.com

SIGNATURE PRODUCT *Holy Chipotle*

NEWEST PRODUCT Raging Passion Pomegranate Habanero Sauce
ADDITIONAL PRODUCTS A full line of hot sauce and hot gourmet
products.

San Angel

668 Worcester Road
Stowe, VT 05672
PHONE (800) 598-6448; E-MAIL dpeet@pwshift

SIGNATURE PRODUCT *Salsa and chips*

NEWEST PRODUCT Verde salsa
ADDITIONAL PRODUCTS Mexican pasta sauce, chipotle pecans

▦ Santa Barbara Olive Co.

3280 Calzada, P.O. Box 1570
Santa Ynez, CA 93460
PHONE (800) 624-4896; FAX (805) 686-1659

Santa Fe Select

410 Old Santa Fe Trail
Santa Fe, NM 87501
PHONE (800) 243-0353

SIGNATURE PRODUCT *Fire Dance Salsa*

NEWEST PRODUCT Apple/Jalapeno jelly
ADDITIONAL PRODUCTS New Mexico apples, red and green halapeno
bits, cactus chipotle salsa, Bonita Roja hot sauce, Hell Raisin'
Habanero

Seyco Fine Foods
970 E Santa Clara Street
Ventura, CA 93001-3033
PHONE (800) 423-2942; FAX (805) 641-9919
WEB SITE http://www.west.net/~adunstan/
E-MAIL adunstan@west.net

Shawnee Canning Co.
212 Cross Junction Road, P.O. Box 657
Cross Junction, VA 22625
PHONE (800) 713-1414; FAX (540) 888-7963
WEB SITE www.w3ic.com/shawnee/
E-MAIL shawcan@crosslink.net

Southwest Specialty Food
5805 W. McLellan Road
Glendale, AZ 85301
PHONE (800) 536-3131; FAX (602) 931-9931
WEB SITE www.asskickin,com
E-MAIL southwest@asskickin.com

SIGNATURE PRODUCT *Asskickin' salsas*

NEWEST PRODUCT Spontaneous Combustion hot sauce and salsa
ADDITIONAL PRODUCTS Salsas, hot sauce, peppers, olives, BBQ
sauce, seasonings from HELL, Three Banditos salsa, Cactus Willy
salsa and hot sauces and seasonings

Spice Merchant
P.O. Box 524
Jackson Hole, WY 83001
PHONE (800) 551-5999; FAX (307) 733-6343
WEB SITE emall.com/spke
E-MAIL 71553.436@compuserve.con

Summerset Ranch

1600 Lupine Lane
Templeton, CA 93465
PHONE (805) 434-2517; FAX (805) 434-2407
WEB SITE www.thegrid.net/summerset_
E-MAIL summersetranch@thegrid.net

SIGNATURE PRODUCT **Pineapple guava chutney and pineapple guava marmalade**

NEWEST PRODUCT Pineapple Guava French Orleans Style Gourmet Vinegar
ADDITIONAL PRODUCTS Cranberry-Pineapple Guava Delight (preserves)

Sunfresh Food Inc. "Freezerves"

125 South Kenyon Street
Seattle, WA 98108
PHONE (800) 669-9625; FAX (206) 764-0960
WEB SITE www.chcs.com/sunfresh; E-MAIL sunfresh@chcs.com

SIGNATURE PRODUCT **Strawberry & raspberry "freezerves"**

NEWEST PRODUCT Assorted cases of raspberry, strawberry, marionberry "freezerve"
ADDITIONAL PRODUCTS Marionberry, seedless raspberry and marionberry, boysenberry and more
COMMENTS *It's amazing how fresh and flavorful these jams/preserves are, I really liked all of them but particularly the marionberry and blueberry. They taste right out of the garden!*

Superbly Southwestern

2400 Rio Grande NW #1-171
Albuquerque, NM 87104
PHONE (800) 467-4HOT
WEB SITE www.hotchile.com
E-MAIL hotchile@aol.com

Taste The Pain
288 Laneda, P.O. Box 554
Manzanita, OR 97130-0554
PHONE (888) 747-PAIN; FAX (888) 747-PAIN
WEB SITE http://www.tastethepain.com
E-MAIL TasteOne@tastethepain.com

SIGNATURE PRODUCT *We are a retail hot sauce (and related products) company*

▩ Tasty Link Inc.
517 Lafayette Avenue
Wyckoff, NJ 07481
PHONE (201) 944-8021; FAX (201) 944-8183
WEB SITE http://www.websternet.com/tasty.html
E-MAIL sales@websternet.com

▩ TECAPP srl
Lungotevere Flaminio 46
Rome Italy 196
PHONE ++396/321.51.15; FAX ++396/321.51.15
WEB SITE http://www.italiantidbits.com
E-MAIL e.romano@agora.stm.it

▩ Timber Crest Farms
4791 Dry Creek Road
Healdsburg, CA 95448
PHONE (707) 433-8251; FAX (707) 433-8255
WEB SITE www.timbercrest.com/tcf/
E-MAIL tcf@timbercrest.com

▩ Tree Mouse Edibles Inc.
RR 4, Site 430 C32
Courtenay, British Columbia CANADA V9N-7J3
PHONE (250) 337-5518; FAX (250) 337-5682
WEB SITE www.vquest.com/treemouse
E-MAIL tremouse@comox.island.net

▓ Twin Peaks Gourmet Trading Post
725 Burnett Avenue #6
San Francisco, CA 94131
PHONE (888) 4TPEAKS (487-3257); FAX (415) 824-7849
WEB SITE   http://tpeaks.com
E-MAIL   gourmet@tpeaks.com

Unlimited Gourmet Foods
Box 16026-3017, Mountain Highway
N. Vancouver, British Columbia CANADA V7J 2R0
PHONE (800) 797-0177; FAX (604) 988-2996
WEB SITE   www.vancouver-bc.com/unlimitedgourmet/index.html
E-MAIL   pwieser@cyberstore.ca

SIGNATURE PRODUCT   **Viniagrettes; raspberry, orange-honey, pink peppercorn**

NEWEST PRODUCT   Herb and garlic
ADDITIONAL PRODUCTS   Blueberry and cranberry viniagrette

▓ Virginia Diner
P.O. Box 1030
Wakefield, VA 23888
PHONE (800) 868-6887; FAX (757) 899-2281
WEB SITE   www.vadiner.com
E-MAIL   vadiner@infi.net

Wax Orchards
22744 Wax Orchards Road, S.W.
Vashon Island, WA 98070
PHONE (800) 634-6132; FAX (206) 463-9731

SIGNATURE PRODUCT   **Oh, Fudge!**

NEWEST PRODUCT   Berry spreads
ADDITIONAL PRODUCTS   Fudge topping: classic fudge, amaretto
    fudge, plus butters, syrups, concentrated fruit juices and condiments
COMMENTS   *All of their products are flavored with concentrated fruit juice
    rather than refined sugar. And still their fudge sauce is great!*

Wescobee Limited

P.O. Box 105
Bayswater Western Australia
Perth, WA 6053 WESTERN AUSTRALIA
PHONE 08 92718133; FAX 08 92711025
WEB SITE http://kite.ois.net.au/~eduard/
E-MAIL eduard@ois.net.au

SIGNATURE PRODUCT **Wescobee Honey**

NEWEST PRODUCT Ezy Serve Honey

Western Trails Inc.

P.O. Box 460
Bozeman, MT 59771
PHONE (800) 759-5489; FAX (406) 587-8087
WEB SITE http://www.gomontana.com/Business/WT/wt.html
E-MAIL westrn@gomontana.com

The Weston Fudge Shop

Route 100, P.O. Box 75
Weston, VT 05161
PHONE (800) 824-3014; FAX (802) 824-3014
WEB SITE www.westonfudge.com

Wood's Cider Mill

RFD #2, Box 477
Springfield, VT 05156
PHONE (802) 263-5547

SIGNATURE PRODUCT **Cider jelly**

NEWEST PRODUCT Cinnamon cider syrup
ADDITIONAL PRODUCTS Maple syrup, boiled cider
COMMENTS *The cider syrup has a nice tangy taste that's a little different than maple syrup and quite nice!*

▦ *Yasmin Gourmet Food*
56 Pleasant Street
Greenville, RI 02828-1920
PHONE (401) 949-2121; FAX (401) 949-0991
WEB SITE   hudson.idt.net/~brbina19/
E-MAIL   bobbybina@hotmail.com

CONFECTIONS

All varieties of candy from chocolates to salt water taffy.

Ann Hemying Candy, Inc. Chocolate Factory
118 North Main Street
Trumbauersville, PA 18970
PHONE (800) 779-7004; FAX (215) 536-6848
WEB SITE   www.chocolateshop.com
E-MAIL   chocolat@fast.net

SIGNATURE PRODUCT   *Over 1,800 chocolate products*

NEWEST PRODUCT   Crunch frogs and golden monkeys
ADDITIONAL PRODUCTS   We have over 1,600 molded novelties from
chocolate ants to the letter "Z." Our chocolates are made by hand and
are very creative. If we don't have a mold, we'll free-form chocolate in
any shape. We have made gazebos, globes, suitcases and more.

Bates Nut Farm
15954 Woodsvalley Road
Valley Center, CA 92082
PHONE (760) 749-3333; FAX (760) 749-9499

Big Betty's
P.O. Box 531
Glenorchy, Tasmania AUSTRALIA 7010
PHONE (61) 36261-3296;   FAX   (61) 36261-3296
WEB SITE   www.ozemail.com.au/~bbetty's
E-MAIL   bbettys@ozemail.com.au

Boehms Chocolates
1101 Supermall Way #1332
Auburn, WA 98001
PHONE (206) 735-1994; FAX (206) 735-1911

WEB SITE www.forsuccess.com/chocolate/boehms
E-MAIL boehms@wolfenet.com

SIGNATURE PRODUCT *Chocolates*

ADDITIONAL PRODUCTS Assorted chocolates from victorian creams,
assorted truffles, nut clusters, candy bars; also toppings and ground
chocolate are available.

Brown & Haley

P.O. Box 1596
Tacoma, WA 98401-1596
PHONE (800) 426-8400; FAX (206) 272-6742
WEB SITE www.brown-haley.com
E-MAIL sweets@brown-haley.com

SIGNATURE PRODUCT *Almond Roca chocolates*

ADDITIONAL PRODUCTS Almond rocas and chocolate truffles, other
candies and gift baskets
COMMENTS *When I was a little girl these were considered the treat of treats. It
is nice that they have remained so, almond rocas are a great candy. If you
don't know them, they should be on your "must try" list.*

California Candy Company

274 Lorton Avenue
Burlingame, CA 94010
PHONE (415) 344-6300; FAX (415) 344-9494
WEB SITE http://californiacandy.com
E-MAIL cheryl@californiacandy.com

SIGNATURE PRODUCT *Candy, Jelly Belly Beans, Novelty Candy*

NEWEST PRODUCT Old Fashioned Hard To Find Candy
ADDITIONAL PRODUCTS Fizzies, Pop Rocks, Nik L Nips, Necco
Wafers, Candy Dots of Paper, Beemans Gum, Clove Gum, Teaberry
Gum, Old Fashioned Taffy, Cinnamon Toothpicks, Zotz, Howards
Scented Gum, Pizie Sticks, Bubble Gum Cigars, Candy Cigarettes,
Walnettos, and more

The Children's Catalog

Children's Home Society of Washington, P.O. Box 15190
Seattle, WA 98115
PHONE (800) 856-5437; FAX (206) 523-1667
WEB SITE www.chs-wa.org

Chocolate Delights

393 Ridgedale Avenue
East Hanover, NJ 07936-1441
PHONE (973) 386-0834
WEB SITE chocolatedelights.com
E-MAIL candy@chocolatedelights.com

SIGNATURE PRODUCT *Chocolate-covered strawberries*

Chocolates by Mark

1039 Del Norte Street
Houston, TX 77018-1422
PHONE (713) 683-3866; FAX (713) 683-3866
WEB SITE www.phoenix.net/~mcaffey; E-MAIL chocolates@4u.net

SIGNATURE PRODUCT *Handmade European-style chocolates*

NEWEST PRODUCT Personalized birth announcement

Chocolates to Die For

6320 Far Hills Avenue
Centerville, OH 45459
PHONE (888) BELCHOC; FAX (937) 435-8420
WEB SITE www.chocolatestodiefor.com
E-MAIL chocolates@2die4.com

SIGNATURE PRODUCT *Fine Belgian Chocolates*

ADDITIONAL PRODUCTS Hand-made, fresh Belgian pralines, truffles, and flavored wafers
COMMENTS *These are more than outstanding chocolates, they are beyond imagination, they're so fantastic . . . and yes, probably even to die for. They are most definitely on my "must try" list.*

Drews Chocolates

426 State Street
Dexter, IA 50070
PHONE (800) 24-DREWS; FAX (515) 789-4540

SIGNATURE PRODUCT   *Fork-dipped chocolates*

ADDITIONAL PRODUCTS   Eight chocolate covered fudges, caramels,
chocolate covered nuts, bars, toffee crunch and famous Drew drops
(caramel and pecans covered in chocolate)

Ethel M Chocolates

P.O. Box 98505
Las Vegas, NV 89193-8505
PHONE (800) 438-4356; FAX (702) 451-8379

SIGNATURE PRODUCT   *Lemon buttercreams/almond butter krisps*

ADDITIONAL PRODUCTS   Cream liqueurs, cherry cordials, mixed fruit
candy, silk truffles, nuts, caramels, and assorted butter creams
COMMENTS   *All the butter creams are my favorite, but then so are the
almond butter krisps. Very nice box of chocolates!*

Farm2You

P.O. Box 9146
Chico, CA 95927
PHONE (888) FARM2YOU; FAX (916) 865-4929
WEB SITE   http://www.farm2you.com
E-MAIL   steve@farm2you.com

Ferris Valley Groves

P.O. Box 530567
Harlingen, TX 78553-0567
PHONE (800) 748-7182; FAX (210) 412-6148
E-MAIL   sarah@valleygroves.com

Flying Fajitas
13710 Chittim Oak
San Antonio, TX 78232
PHONE (800) 290-3411
WEB SITE www.fajitas.com
E-MAIL Flyingfajitas@stic.net

Gifts from the Illinois Amish Country
138 S. Vine
Arthur, IL 61911
PHONE (800) 879-2494; FAX (217) 543-2898
WEB SITE www.IllinoisAmishCountry.com/WLPantry/gifthome.htm
E-MAIL AmishCM@net66.com

SIGNATURE PRODUCT **Aunt Sarah's Fudge**

NEWEST PRODUCT Regular or sucrose-free Amish Fruit Spreads in gift
boxes
ADDITIONAL PRODUCTS Illinois Amish jams, jellies and fruit butters
individually or in gift baskets. Illinois Amish candies individually or in
baskets. Most of the above items available sucrose-free; Amish cheese
assortments and gift baskets
COMMENTS *I particularly liked the Dutch apple butter.*

Glade Candy Co.
dba: Taffy Town
55 West 800 South
Salt Lake City, UT 84101
PHONE (801) 355-4637; FAX (801) 355-7664
WEB SITE www.TaffyTown.com
E-MAIL Worlds_Best_Taffy@TaffyTown.com

SIGNATURE PRODUCT **Taffy Town Brand: Salt Water Taffy**

NEWEST PRODUCT Sassy Taffy (sour taffy)
ADDITIONAL PRODUCTS We manufacture over 50 single flavors and
designs of Salt Water Taffy in both packaged and bulk.
COMMENTS *It's taffy. And it's good.*

GOODIES Express
6510 S. Xenon Street
Littleton, CO 80127
PHONE (888) 904-1923; FAX (303) 904-1921
WEB SITE http://www.goodiesexpress.com
E-MAIL lynnzy@goodiesexpress.com

The Gourmet Padre
405 W. Cloverhurst Avenue
Athens, GA 30606
PHONE (800) 43-PADRE; FAX (706) 543-7557
WEB SITE www/gourmet-padre.com
E-MAIL gpadre@negia.com

SIGNATURE PRODUCT *Posh pecans*

ADDITIONAL PRODUCTS Candies, cakes, fudge, and cheesecake
COMMENTS *Lovely candies, particularly liked the frangelico posh pecan.*

Great American Popcorn Company
311 S. Main Street
Galena, IL 61036
PHONE (800) 814-9494; FAX (815) 777-4118
WEB SITE www.popcorn.com
E-MAIL popcorn1.galenalink.com

Great Food Online
2030 1st Avenue, 3rd Floor
Seattle, WA 98121
PHONE (800) 841-5984; FAX (206) 443-3314
WEB SITE http://www.greatfood.com
E-MAIL proprietor@greatfood.com

Green Mountain Sugar House
Box 82, Route 100N
Ludlow, VT 05149
PHONE (800) 643-9338; FAX (802) 228-2298
E-MAIL gmsh@ludl.tds.net

Harbor Sweets

85 Leavitt Street, Palmer Cove
Salem, MA 1970
PHONE (800) 243-2115; FAX (508) 741-7811
E-MAIL hsweets@shore.net

SIGNATURE PRODUCT **Sweet Sloops**

NEWEST PRODUCT Golf Collection
ADDITIONAL PRODUCTS Four Product lines: Classic Nautical Line
including Sweet Sloops & Sand Dollars (dark chocolate w/caramel
and pecan, Sweet Shells (dark chocolate with orange crunch) and
Harbor Lights (our "truffle" with raspberry & cranberry ganache)
COMMENTS *This is outstanding chocolate both in taste and presentation. I
recommend Harbor Sweets and definitely put them on the "must try" list.*

Haven's Candies

87 County Road
Westbrook, ME 04092
PHONE (800) 639-6309; FAX (207) 774-1884
WEB SITE www.havens-candies.com
E-MAIL havens@mail.biddeford.com

SIGNATURE PRODUCT **Chocolates**

ADDITIONAL PRODUCTS Salt Water taffy, specialty molding, roasted
nuts, fudge, sugar-free chocolates
COMMENTS *I liked the chocolate truffle and the French mint truffle in dark
chocolate.*

Heaton Pecan Farm

309 Sunrise Boulevard
Clanton, AL 35045
PHONE (800) 446-3531; FAX (205) 755-8677

Heavenly Cheesecakes & Chocolates Inc.
1369 Ridgewood Avenue
Holly Hill, FL 32117
PHONE (904) 673-6670; FAX (904) 673-2367
WEB SITE www.heavenlycheesecakes.com
E-MAIL Heavenlycheesecakes@juno.com

The Homestead Sugar House
11393 Homestead Road
Beulah, MI 49617
PHONE (616) 882-7712

How Sweet It Is!
P.O. Box 376
Jenkintown, PA 19046
PHONE (215) 784-9980; FAX (215) 784-0761
WEB SITE www.howsweet.com
E-MAIL tomgold@vikingcomputers.com

SIGNATURE PRODUCT *Gourmet & Custom-Made Chocolate*

NEWEST PRODUCT Custom Corporate Chocolate
ADDITIONAL PRODUCTS Gift Packages — Gourmet sugarfree or low-fat, hard-to-find candy of any type, custom labeled individual candies, cookies; sugarfree & regular nuts; plain or chocolate-covered dried fruit; plain or chocolate-covered pretzels

How Sweet It Is Fudge & Candy Co.!
2275 South M-33
West Branch, MI 48661
PHONE (517) 272-9702; FAX (517) 272-9704
WEB SITE www.sweetfudge.com

SIGNATURE PRODUCT *Handmade fudge*

NEWEST PRODUCT Sugarfree candy selection
ADDITIONAL PRODUCTS Handmade crafts

Karl Bissinger French Confections

3983 Gratiot Street
St. Louis, MO 63110
PHONE (800) 325-8881; FAX (314) 534-2419

SIGNATURE PRODUCT *Chocolate, chocolate-covered raspberries*

NEWEST PRODUCT   Chocolate
ADDITIONAL PRODUCTS   Chocolate caramels, nuts, truffles, English
   toffee, chocolate-dipped fruit, clusters, barks, mints, chocolate nonpareils, marzipan, molasses chips, puffs, caramels, pecan nut balls,
   French coconut, cordials, coffee, chocolates, etc.
COMMENTS   *Classic good chocolate candies. Wish I'd been able to sample
   their very precious (available only for three weeks) chocolate-dipped raspberries, but what I had was great!*

Lambs Farm

P.O. Box 520
Libertyville, IL 60048
PHONE (800) 52-LAMBS; FAX (847) 362-6319

Lammes Candies

P.O. Box 1885
Austin, TX 78767-1885
PHONE (800) 252-1885; FAX (512) 310-2280
WEB SITE   www.lammes.com

SIGNATURE PRODUCT   *"Texas Chewie" pecan pralines*

NEWEST PRODUCT   Peanut paws
ADDITIONAL PRODUCTS   Longhorns, choc'adillos, cashew critters,
   taffy kisses, pecan divinity, assorted chocolates, peanut pardners
COMMENTS   *Very nice pralines; the Longhorns were my favorite.*

Mack's Groves

1180 North Federal Highway
Pompano Beach, FL 33062
PHONE (800) 327-3525; FAX (954) 942-1463
WEB SITE   www.webpc.com/macks/; E-MAIL macks@gate.net

▩ Madly Pop'n

148 N. Oak Park Avenue
Oak Park, IL 60301
PHONE (800) 774-5620; FAX (708) 386-7904
WEB SITE www.madlypopn.com
E-MAIL rachel@madlypopn.com

▩ Manhattan Fruitier

105 East 29th Street
New York, NY 10016
PHONE (800) 841-5718; FAX (212) 689-0479
WEB SITE www.nystyle.com/manfruit
E-MAIL manfruit@nystyle.com

▩ Mary of Puddin Hill

4007 Interstate 30, P.O. Box 241
Greensville, TX 75403-0241
PHONE (800) 545-8889; FAX (903) 455-4522

▩ Mauna Loa Macadamia Nuts

6523 North Galena Road, P.O. Box 1772
Peoria, IL 61656
PHONE (800) 832-9993; FAX (309) 689-3893
WEB SITE www.maunaloa.com

▩ Mixon Fruit Farms Inc.

2712 26th Avenue E
Bradenton, FL 34208
PHONE (800) 608-2525; FAX (941) 748-1085
WEB SITE www.mixon.com
E-MAIL Info@mixon.com

▩ Only Gourmet

P.O. Box 2214
Orinda, CA 94563
PHONE (888) 413-6637; FAX (510) 531-4981
WEB SITE http://www.onlygourmet.com
E-MAIL alank@onlygourmet.com

▦ ORE-ASIA
4651 NE Riverside Drive
McMinnville, OR 97128
PHONE (503) 434-9766; FAX (503) 434-2809
WEB SITE www.ore-asia.com
E-MAIL info@ore-asia.com

Pierre Vivier

WEB SITE www.pvchocolates.com
E-MAIL vivier@polaris.net

SIGNATURE PRODUCT **Fine chocolates**

COMMENTS *This is absolutely extraordinary chocolate. Very unusual and creative chocolates that are definitely high on the "must try" list. And, yes, the only way you can order them is on the internet.*

▦ POP 'N STUFF INC.
Broadway at the Beach, 1303 Celebrity Circle 125
Myrtle Beach, SC 29577
PHONE (800) 735-5440; FAX (803) 946-6813
WEB SITE http://sccoast.net/popn/popnstuf/home.htm:
E-MAIL popn@sccoast.net

Queen Square Delicatessen
20 Queen Square
Cambridge, Ontario CANADA N1S-1H3
PHONE (888) 230-2656; FAX (519) 622-2613
WEB SITE www.queensquare.com
E-MAIL info@queensquare.com

SIGNATURE PRODUCT **British candy and grocery items**

NEWEST PRODUCT Selection Boxes for Christmas
ADDITIONAL PRODUCTS Flake bars; Fry's Ice Cream; Turkish Delight; Galaxy Bars; Minstrel's Club Bars, Penguins; Topics Milky Bars; Milky Buttons, nougat bars; Sherbert Fountains; Mars Bars; Lion Bars; fudge; treackle pudding and more

Rocky Mountain Chocolate Factory

▐▋▐

207 South Main
Galena, IL 61036
PHONE (800) 235-8160; FAX (888) BY-ROCKY
WEB SITE www.rockymtchoc.com
E-MAIL rockymt@galenalink.com

SIGNATURE PRODUCT *Rocky Mountain Chocolate Bears and Truffles*

ADDITIONAL PRODUCTS   Nut clusters, peanut butter cups, toffee,
    dipped apples, bark, dipped pretzels, graham crackers, dipped fruit,
    sugar-free candy, gift boxes of fudge
COMMENTS   *Rocky Mountain was unable to ship chocolate due to a heat
    wave; but I did sample their fudge and it was very good, suspect their choco-
    lates are, too!*

Rowena's

758 West 22nd Street
Norfolk, VA 23517
PHONE (800) 627-8699; FAX (804) 627-1505
WEB SITE pilotonline.com/Rowena's; E-MAIL Rowena's@aol.com

Seyco Fine Foods

970 E Santa Clara Street
Ventura, CA 93001-3033
PHONE (800) 423-2942; FAX (805) 641-9919
WEB SITE http://www.west.net/~adunstan/
E-MAIL adunstan@west.net

Shelton-Mathews Chocolates

2503 Mahoning Avenue
Youngstown, OH 44509
PHONE (800) 844-9497; FAX (330) 799-0889
WEB SITE www.cisnet.com/chocolates

SIGNATURE PRODUCT *Gourmet chocolates*

ADDITIONAL PRODUCTS   Exquisite chocolates: white and dark
    ganache, Belgian praline, dresse noix, and noisette, raspberry, mocha,

orange, and cognac

▣ *Stahmann's*
P.O. Box 130
San Miguel, NM 88058-0130
PHONE (800) 654-6887; FAX (505) 526-7824
WEB SITE www.stahmanns.com

▣ *Sutton Place Gourmet*
10323 Old Georgetown Road
Bethesda, MD 20814
PHONE (800) 346-8763; FAX (301) 564-3016
WEB SITE www.suttongourmet
E-MAIL concierge@suttongourmet.com

Tasty Link Inc.
517 Lafayette Avenue
Wyckoff, NJ 07481
PHONE (201) 944-8021; FAX (201) 944-8183
WEB SITE http://www.websternet.com/tasty.html
E-MAIL sales@websternet.com

SIGNATURE PRODUCT **Boca Bons**

NEWEST PRODUCT Godiva
ADDITIONAL PRODUCTS Chocolate Cigars, It's a Boy/Girl Cigars, Chocolate Champagne Bottles, Brandy Balls, custom baked in any shape cookies, Bernardaud Collection from France (tea/jams/etc.), Boca Bons in assorted sizes

Topographic Chocolate Company
2601 Blake Street
Denver, CO 80205
PHONE (800) 779-8985; FAX (303) 292-6365
WEB SITE topochocolate.com
E-MAIL toponet@msn.com

SIGNATURE PRODUCT **Chocolate boxes**

NEWEST PRODUCT   Chocolate dinosaurs
ADDITIONAL PRODUCTS   Hand-foil wrapped chocolate novelties, specialty mold, solid chocolate pieces and customized chocolates with corporate logos

Trappistine Quality Candy

Mt. St. Mary's Abbey, 300 Arnold Street
Wrentham, MA 02093-1799
PHONE (508) 528-1282; FAX (508) 528-1409
WEB SITE   www.xmission.com/~arts/abbey/
E-MAIL   haze@ultranet.com

SIGNATURE PRODUCT   **Butternut munch**

NEWEST PRODUCT   Almond bark
ADDITIONAL PRODUCTS   Fudge with walnuts, penuche, chocolate-covered caramels
COMMENTS   *Heavenly candy, of course!*

Virginia Diner

P.O. Box 1030
Wakefield, VA 23888
PHONE (800) 868-6887; FAX (757) 899-2281
WEB SITE   www.vadiner.com; E-MAIL   vadiner@infi.net

Wertz Candies Inc.

718 Cumberland Street
Lebanon, PA 17042
PHONE (717) 273-0511; FAX (717) 273-0623
WEB SITE   www.wertzcandy.com; E-MAIL wertz@nbn.net

SIGNATURE PRODUCT   **Opera Fudge**

NEWEST PRODUCT   Chocolate-covered caramel dipped pretzels
ADDITIONAL PRODUCTS   Big Block Marshmallow (in milk or dark chocolate), assorted truffles in light or dark chocolate, creams of all varieties; our own nonpareils; our own caramels in vanilla or chocolate
COMMENTS   *Nice chocolates!*

The Weston Fudge Shop
Route 100, P.O. Box 75
Weston, VT 05161
PHONE (800) 824-3014; FAX (802) 824-3014
WEB SITE   www.westonfudge.com

SIGNATURE PRODUCT   *Fudge*

ADDITIONAL PRODUCTS   A variety of hand-dipped chocolates, hot
fudge sauce in many flavors as well as many different fudges

COMMENTS   *Who could not love a good rich chocolate fudge sauce? And this
one is great.*

DAIRY PRODUCTS

Cheeses from goat cheese chevre to cheddar, mozzarella, Parmesan and mascarpone; also creme fraiche and quark.

Alto Dairy
307 N. Clark Street
Black Creek, WI 54106
PHONE (920) 984-3331 ext. 327; FAX (920) 984-3926

SIGNATURE PRODUCT **Cheddar cheese (aged)**

ADDITIONAL PRODUCTS Colby, rindless brick, Monterey Jack, Col-brick, mozzarella, edam, pepper Jack, caraway cheddar, garlic cheddar

Bandon's Cheese
680 East 2nd, P.O. Box 1668
Bandon, OR 97411
PHONE (800) 548-8961; FAX (541) 347-2012

SIGNATURE PRODUCT **Full cream extra sharp cheddar**

NEWEST PRODUCT Organic cheddar
ADDITIONAL PRODUCTS Many types of cheddars, plus gift baskets

Bass Lake Cheese Factory
598 Valley View Trail
Somerset, WI 54025
PHONE (715) 247-5586; Fax (715) 549-6617

SIGNATURE PRODUCT **Specialty cheese**

NEWEST PRODUCT Muenster Delray - Mezcla Kassari (cow/sheep milks)
ADDITIONAL PRODUCTS Fifty-two different types of cheese, handmade from cow, sheep or goat's milk. No additives or preservatives are used.

Calef's Country Store

Route 9, P.O. Box 57
Barrington, NH 03825
PHONE (603) 664-2231; FAX (603) 664-5857
WEB SITE www.wertzcandy.com
E-MAIL wertz@nbn.net

SIGNATURE PRODUCT *Snappy old cheese*

ADDITIONAL PRODUCTS Lots of old-fashioned products such as jams
    and jellies, baked beans and pancake mixes
COMMENTS *The snappy old cheese is a great sharp cheddar!*

Caroline Kountry Gold

774 Main Street, P.O. Box 136
Caroline, WI 54928-0137
PHONE (715) 754-2445; FAX (715) 754-4835
WEB SITE www.frontiercomm.net/~fkostlev/gold.html
E-MAIL fkostlev@wi.frontiercomm.net

SIGNATURE PRODUCT *Cheese*

NEWEST PRODUCT Sharp cheddar cheese crocks
ADDITIONAL PRODUCTS Cheddar and other cheeses in varying sizes
    and shapes, spreads and gift boxes
COMMENTS *It's cheddar cheese!*

Crowley Cheese

Healdville Road
Healdville, VT 05758
PHONE (800) 683-2606; FAX (802) 259-2347

SIGNATURE PRODUCT *Cheese*

NEWEST PRODUCT More cheese
ADDITIONAL PRODUCTS Extra-sharp, sharp, mild, medium sharp,
    smoked, garlic, onion, caraway, dill, sage, and hot pepper
COMMENTS *Cheese is what they do, and only cheese . . . so they're quite
    good at it. I like the garlic cheese the best.*

DiBruno Bros. House of Cheese

930 South 9th Street
Philadelphia, PA 19147
PHONE (888) 322-4337; FAX (215) 922-2080
WEB SITE http://www.dibruno.com
E-MAIL dibruno@gim.net

SIGNATURE PRODUCT **Reggiano Parmigiano - Aged cheeses**

ADDITIONAL PRODUCTS Homemade cheese spreads; extra virgin
olive oil, aged balsamic vinegar, gourmet meats, olives, over 500
cheeses from around the world, coffee, handmade pasta and many
more gourmet specialty items
COMMENTS *These cheese spreads are exceptional and I think they should be
on the "must try" list.*

▦ Dave's Gourmet Inc.

1255 Montgomery Avenue
San Bruno, CA 94066
PHONE (800) 758-0372; FAX (415) 794-0340
WEB SITE davesgourmet.com
E-MAIL insanity@davesgourmet.com

Gethsemani Farms

3642 Monks Road
Trappist, KY 40051
PHONE (502) 549-4138; FAX (502) 549-4124
WEB SITE www.monks.org

SIGNATURE PRODUCT **Trappist cheese**

NEWEST PRODUCT Trappist Bourbon Fudge
ADDITIONAL PRODUCTS Trappist Bourbon Fruitcake
COMMENTS *The Brothers may say that they are best-known for their fine
cheeses (and they are good), but it is their fruitcake that is truly heavenly
and like none other. This is on the "must try" list.*

▦ Gifts from the Illinois Amish Country

138 S. Vine
Arthur, IL 61911
PHONE (800) 879-2494; FAX (217) 543-2898
WEB SITE www.IllinoisAmishCountry.com/WLPantry/gifthome.htm
E-MAIL AmishCM@net66.com

Harman's Cheese & Country

1400 Route 117
Sugar Hill, NH 03585
PHONE (603) 823-8000; FAX (603) 823-8000

SIGNATURE PRODUCT **Aged cheddar cheese**

ADDITIONAL PRODUCTS Cheese spreads, maple products, preserves,
 smoked salmon, crabmeat, baskets, gourmet foods
COMMENTS *I really liked their cheese spread, very nice flavor.*

▦ Manganaro Foods

488 Ninth Avenue
New York, NY 10018
PHONE (800) 4-SALAMI; FAX (212) 239-8355

Maple Leaf Cheese Factory

W2616, Hwy 11-81
Juda, WI 53550
PHONE (608) 934-1237; FAX (608) 934-1239

SIGNATURE PRODUCT *Traditional "wheel" Monterey Jack*

NEWEST PRODUCT Raw milk cheddar
ADDITIONAL PRODUCTS Gouda, cheddars up to two years, pesto
 Monterey Jack, salsa Jack, veggie Jack, caraway Jack and smoked gouda
COMMENTS *The Jacks were very nice but I particularly liked the gouda, a
 very nice cheese indeed.*

Maytag Dairy Farms

P.O. Box 806
Newton, IA 50208
PHONE (800) 247-2458; FAX (515) 792-1567

SIGNATURE PRODUCT   *Maytag Blue Cheese*

NEWEST PRODUCT   White cheddar
ADDITIONAL PRODUCTS   Edam, baby Swiss, regular Swiss, brick;
cheddar and blue cheese spreads

Meister Cheese Co.

1050 E. Nebraska Street, P.O. Box 68
Muscoda, WI 53573
PHONE (800) MEISTER; FAX (608) 739-4348
WEB SITE   www.meistercheese.com
E-MAIL   bigcheez@meistercheese.com

SIGNATURE PRODUCT   *Grandpa Meister's Wisconsin Specialty Cheese*

NEWEST PRODUCT   Great Plains Flavored Monterey Jacks
ADDITIONAL PRODUCTS   Hundreds of different types of cheeses in all
shapes and sizes
COMMENTS   *I liked the jalapeno Jack.*

Nordic House

3421 Telegraph Avenue
Oakland, CA 94609
PHONE (800) 854-6435; FAX (510) 653-1936
WEB SITE   nordichouse.com
E-MAIL   pia@nordichouse.com

Pasta Just For You By Sue

111 West Main
West Dundee, IL 60118
PHONE (800) PASTA-US; FAX (847) 836-1014

Steve's Cheese Co.

220 S. Bohemia Drive, P.O. Box 385
Denmark, WI 54208
PHONE (888) 427-0483; FAX (920) 863-8930
WEB SITE www.stevescheese.com
E-MAIL steves@stevescheese.com

SIGNATURE PRODUCT *Parmesan cheese and white cheddar*

NEWEST PRODUCT Pepato (romano-like), Larry's string cheese
ADDITIONAL PRODUCTS Steve's handles the full line of Bel Gioioso
Cheese which includes: romano, asiago, kasseri, fontina, gorganzola,
auribella, mascarpone, provolone, and more; their own cheeses including cheddar, Colby, Swiss, Monterey Jack, brick, mozzarella and more
COMMENTS *I've tried the Bel Gioioso cheeses and they are fantastic, particularly the provolone and gorganzola, and now their newest pepato. And Steve's
makes their own great mozzarella and cheddar. On the "must try" list.*

Tillamook Cheese

4175 Hwy 101 N, P.O. Box 313
Tillamook, OR 97141
PHONE (800) 542-7290; FAX (503) 815-1305

SIGNATURE PRODUCT *Cheddar cheese*

ADDITIONAL PRODUCTS Sharp, aged; extra-sharp; and medium aged
cheddars in several sizes. Also gift baskets which include Tillamook
cheese and other "Northwestern" products
CATALOG INFO Attractive catalog
COMMENTS *Very nice, straight-forward cheddar cheese.*

Vella Cheese

315 Second Street East, P.O. Box 191
Sonoma, CA 95476
PHONE (707) 938-3232; FAX (707) 938-4307
WEB SITE www.vellacheese.com/
E-MAIL vella@vom.com

SIGNATURE PRODUCT   *Dry Jack cheese*

NEWEST PRODUCT   Asiago and Rosemary Jack
ADDITIONAL PRODUCTS   Cheddar cheeses, and Jack cheeses; plain or
seasoned with both

Vermont Butter & Cheese
Pitman Road, P.O. Box 95
Websterville, VT 05678
PHONE (800) VT-GOATS; FAX (802) 479-3674

SIGNATURE PRODUCT   *Vermont chevre and chevrier*

NEWEST PRODUCT   Vermont fontina (an aged goats' milk cheese)
ADDITIONAL PRODUCTS   Cow's milk cheeses: creme fraiche, mascarpone, fromage blanc, quark, basil torta, salmon torte, cultured butter.
Also, goats milk cheeses: chevre, cheddar, chevrier, fontina, impastata
COMMENTS   *Absolutely fabulous goats' cheese! Really worth going out of
your way for. I also love the quark, impastata and creme fraiche. This is on
the "must try" list.*

Washington State University Creamery
101 Food Quality Building, P.O. Box 646392
Pullman, WA 99164-6392
PHONE (800) 457-5442; FAX (800) 572-3289
WEB SITE   www.wsu.edu/creamery
E-MAIL   creamery@wsu.edu

SIGNATURE PRODUCT   *Cougar Gold Cheese*

NEWEST PRODUCT   Cracked Pepper & Chive Cheese
ADDITIONAL PRODUCTS   All products are 30 oz. cans of cheese:
American cheddar, smoky cheddar, dill garlic, viking, sweet basil, hot
pepper, Italian, reduced fat viking

GRAINS & FLOURS

Flours, pancake mixes, wild rice and tortillas and tortilla chips.

1-800-GRANOLA
P.O. Box 756
Amherst, MA 01004
PHONE (800) GRANOLA
WEB SITE www.800granola.com
E-MAIL info@800granola.com

SIGNATURE PRODUCT **Granola**

ADDITIONAL PRODUCTS Granola and muesli cereals, snacks and trail mixes, bars, nuts and seeds, and samplers

Bernard Food Industries
3540 W. Jarvis Avenue
Skokie, IL 60204
PHONE (800) 325-5409; FAX (847) 679-5417
WEB SITE www.diet-shoppe.com

Bette's Diner Products

1807 Fourth Street
Berkeley, CA 94710
PHONE (510) 644-3932; FAX (510) 644-3209
WEB SITE bettesdiner.com
E-MAIL bette@dnai.com

SIGNATURE PRODUCT **Pancake mixes**

NEWEST PRODUCT Four-grain Buttermilk Pancake Mix
ADDITIONAL PRODUCTS Mixes for scones, pancake handbook, coffees
COMMENTS *These are delightful products; both the scones and oatmeal pancake mixes were fun and easy to use, plus delicious. I'd love to go to the diner the next time I'm in California, very funky looking!*

Boo-Daddy's Chile Pepper Company

P.O. Box 6245
North Augusta, SC 29861-6245
PHONE (800) 436-6794; FAX (706) 790-9898
WEB SITE www.augusta.net/boo_daddy's/
E-MAIL Rkeller@augusta.net

The Bread Basket L.L.C.

2116 Taft Highway
Signal Mountain, TN 37377
PHONE (800) 581-0339; FAX (423) 886-9332
WEB SITE http://www.breadbasket.com; E-MAIL bread@voy.net

Cafe Beaujolais Bakery

961 Ukiah Street, P.O. Box 730
Mendocino, CA 95460
PHONE (800) 930-0443; FAX (707) 937-3656
WEB SITE www.cafebeaujolais.com; E-MAIL cafebeau@men.org

Farm2You

P.O. Box 9146
Chico, CA 95927
PHONE (888) FARM2YOU; FAX (916) 865-4929
WEB SITE http://www.farm2you.com
E-MAIL steve@farm2you.com

SIGNATURE PRODUCT **Lundberg Farms organic and gourmet rice varieties**

NEWEST PRODUCT Grande Truffles (1/4 lb. of chocolate indulgence)
ADDITIONAL PRODUCTS Processed/roasted/flavored nuts; specialty nut products; dried fruits; snacks; candies and specialty rice products.

Flying Noodle

1 Arrowhead Road
Duxbury, MA 02332
PHONE (800) 566-0599; FAX (617) 934-1527
WEB SITE www.flyingnoodle.com

E-MAIL   bigparmesan@flyingnoodle.com

SIGNATURE PRODUCT   *Pasta Club*

ADDITIONAL PRODUCTS   Various pastas; sauces; fresh spinach, garlic,
    ginger, onion vegetables, and basil; oils, broths, Italian condiments
    and lots of gift baskets
COMMENTS   *These were great products, really fun. Of course I liked the
    pasta. The most interesting and unusual is the Sunja's Oriental Sauce,
    which I use continually on cold, left-over pasta (yes, occassionally there's
    some left). Great!*

Gray's Grist Mill
P.O. Box 422
Adamsville, RI 02801
PHONE (508) 636-6075

SIGNATURE PRODUCT   *Rhode Island Johnny cake meal*

ADDITIONAL PRODUCTS   Stoned ground flours from organic grains,
    corn, wheat and rye

Hearty Mix Co.
1231 Madison Hill Road
Rahway, NJ 07065
PHONE   (908) 382-3010

SIGNATURE PRODUCT   *Buttermilk bread mix*

NEWEST PRODUCT   Barley soup mix
Additional products   EStra-Hearty Bread Mixes, good in bread machines
    — buttermilk, whole wheat, Italian, rye, salt rising. Mixes for muffins,
    pancakes, doughnuts, cookies, cakes. Also whole wheat, gluten-free,
    lactose-free, salt-free mixes. No artificial preservatives.
COMMENTS   *The buttermilk bread was very nice but I really liked the brown-
    ie mix, plus both were quick and easy to make.*

Hungry Bear Hemp Foods

P.O. Box 12175
Eugene, OR 97440
PHONE (541) 767-3811; FAX (541) 767-3811
WEB SITE www.efn.org/~gordon_k/Hungrybear.html
E-MAIL eathemp@efn.org

SIGNATURE PRODUCT **Seedy Sweeties**

NEWEST PRODUCT Hemp seed butter
ADDITIONAL PRODUCTS Hemp seed flour, hemp & whole wheat
pancake mix, hemp & whole wheat baking mix, hemp seed oil, hemp
seeds (sterilized), hemp seeds (non-sterilized pressed seeds)

Jane Butel's Pecos Valley Spice

2429 Monroe Street, N.E.
Albuquerque, NM 87110
PHONE (800) 473-TACO; FAX (505) 888-4269

Konriko

307 Ann Street, P.O. Box 10640
New Iberia, LA 70560
PHONE (800) 551-3245; FAX (318) 365-5806

SIGNATURE PRODUCT **Wild pecan rice**

NEWEST PRODUCT Jalepeno all-purpose seasoning
ADDITIONAL PRODUCTS 20 varieties of rice mixes, Hol-grain brown
rice crackers, seasoning products, rice and popcorn cakes
COMMENTS *Yes! It's nice rice!*

Los Chileros de Nuevo Mexico

P.O. Box 6215
Sante Fe, NM 87502
PHONE (505) 471-6967; FAX (505) 473-7306
WEB SITE www.hotchilepepper.com/ordering.htm

Marmix Company

P.O. Box 1458
Newport Beach, CA 92659-0458
PHONE (888) 627-4649; FAX (714) 673-1927
WEB SITE www.marimix.com

Miguel's Stowe Away

RR3, Box 2086
Waterbury, VT 05676
PHONE (800) 448-6517; FAX (802) 244-7804
E-MAIL miguels@together.net

Pasta Just For You By Sue

111 West Main
West Dundee, IL 60118
PHONE (800) PASTA-US; FAX (847) 836-1014

SIGNATURE PRODUCT **Pastas**

ADDITIONAL PRODUCTS Pasta club; 33 flavors of pasta, 8 luscious
sauces, 4 cheeses, 4 breads, and 5 salads. Plus 10 different pasta shapes

Piquant Pepper

P.O. Box 20196
Wichita, KS 67208-1196
PHONE (800) 931-7474; FAX (316) 685-9144
WEB SITE www.shipnizzy.com; E-MAIL piquant@dtc.net

Rossi Pasta Factory Inc.

114 Greene Street, P.O. Box 759
Marietta, OH 45750
PHONE (800) 227-6774;   FAX (614) 373-5310
WEB SITE www.civic.net/webmarket/ then select Rossi Pasta
E-MAIL 102121.2140@compuserve.com

SIGNATURE PRODUCT **25 handmade pastas, 8 homemade red pasta
sauces**

NEWEST PRODUCT Portabella mushroom red pasta sauce

ADDITIONAL PRODUCTS   We also make four no-parboil, flavored lasagna noodles, a tri-color rotini and an assortment of cooking utensils.
COMMENTS   *These were really wonderful products, lovely quality and fine tasting. I liked the spinach-basil-garlic pasta.*

 San Angel
668 Worcester Road
Stowe, VT 05672
PHONE (800) 598-6448
E-MAIL   dpeet@pwshift

Seviroli Foods

601 Brook Street
Garden City, NY 11530
PHONE (800) 866-6215; FAX (516) 222-0534
WEB SITE   www.seviroli.com; E-MAIL   seviroli@idt.net

SIGNATURE PRODUCT   **Tortellini & ravioli**

NEWEST PRODUCT   Prepared Gourmet Pasta Dishes
ADDITIONAL PRODUCTS   Manicotti, stuffed shells, cavatelli, ravioletti, gnocchi
COMMENTS   *Great frozen pasta!*

Southfork Rice Co.

HCR 78 Box 142
Pine River, MN 56474
PHONE (800) 920-2473; FAX (218) 947-3967
WEB SITE   http://www.uslink.net/~flyaird/rice.html
E-MAIL   flyaird@uslink.net

SIGNATURE PRODUCT   **100% hand picked "Wild Rice"**

 Sultan's Delight
P.O. Box 090302
Brooklyn, NY 11209
PHONE (800) 852-5046; FAX (718) 745-2563

Theld Trading Company

P.O. Box 570
LaRonge, Saskatchuan CANADA SOJ IL0
PHONE (800) 780-5473; FAX (306) 425-5514

SIGNATURE PRODUCT **Canadian wild rice**

NEWEST PRODUCT Wild rice kit — herbs and almonds
ADDITIONAL PRODUCTS Wild rice pancake mix, wild rice pasta, wild
   rice flour — all products in varying sizes

Tree Mouse Edibles Inc.

RR 4 Site 430 C32
Courtenay, British Columbia CANADA V9N-7J3
PHONE (250) 337-5518; FAX (250) 337-5682
WEB SITE www.vquest.com/treemouse
E-MAIL tremouse@comox.island.net

Western Trails Inc.

P.O. Box 460
Bozeman, MT 59771
PHONE (800) 759-5489; FAX (406) 587-8087
WEB SITE http://www.gomontana.com/Business/WT/wt.html
E-MAIL westrn@gomontana.com

SIGNATURE PRODUCT **Hulless NuBarley**

NEWEST PRODUCT Cowboy Flapjack Mix
ADDITIONAL PRODUCTS Hulless NuBarley bread, flapjack & soup
   mixes (using hulless barleys and dry beans); cereals (hot); whole grains,
   three types of hulless barleys: Treasure State Nubarley, Bronze Nugget
   NuBarley and Black Buffalo NuBarley plus cowboy beans and sauces
COMMENTS *I liked the flapjack mix; very hefty and flavorful.*

FRUITS

Every variety of fresh fruit from mangos to pears and also dried fruit and preserves.

AlpineAire Foods
P.O. Box 926
Nevada City, CA 95959
PHONE (800) FAB-MEAL; FAX (916) 272-2624

American Spoon Foods, Inc.
1668 Clarion Avenue, P.O. Box 566
Petoskey, MI 49770
PHONE (800) 222-5886; FAX (616) 347-2512
WEB SITE www.spoon.com
E-MAIL information@spoon.com

SIGNATURE PRODUCT **Fruit spreads**

ADDITIONAL PRODUCTS Fruit preserves, jellies, jams, fruit butters, dried fruit, trail mix, salad dressings, sauces, mustards, relishes, salsa, dried mushrooms, pancake mix, nuts, and assorted gift baskets
COMMENTS *Their Black Cherry Spoon Fruit remains my absolute favorite, it's the best!*

Apples-N-Such
1245 Stratford Road
Delaware, OH 43015
PHONE (614) 363-1330; FAX (614) 363-5967
WEB SITE http://www.kokodir.com/Apples.html
E-MAIL apples@midohio.net

SIGNATURE PRODUCT **Dried fruits with no preservatives or oils added**

Bates Nut Farm
15954 Woodsvalley Road
Valley Center, CA 92082
PHONE (760) 749-3333; FAX (760) 749-9499

Blood's Hammock Groves
4600 Linton Boulevard
Delray Beach, FL 33445
PHONE (800) 255-5188; FAX (561) 498-0285
WEB SITE   www.bhgcitrus.com; E-MAIL blood's@bhgcitrus.com

SIGNATURE PRODUCT   *Tree-ripened citrus fruit*

NEWEST PRODUCT   Home-made marmalades and other preserves
made from Florida citrus
ADDITIONAL PRODUCTS   Gift baskets, gourmet foods with citrus and
tropical fruit flavors, gifts with Florida flair, juicers and citrus utensils
COMMENTS   *At first I was disappointed that the fresh citrus season was over
and I was unable to sample, but then I was sent the marmalade. The mango
is superb! A "must try."*

The Children's Catalog
Children's Home Society of Washington, P.O. Box 15190
Seattle, WA 98115
PHONE (800) 856-5437; FAX (206) 523-1667
WEB SITE   www.chs-wa.org

SIGNATURE PRODUCT   *Apples*

NEWEST PRODUCT   Sweet cherries
ADDITIONAL PRODUCTS   Pears, smoked salmon, scone mix, Walla-
Walla sweet onions, coffees, holiday wreathes, combo gifts of apples,
pears, cheeses, gourmet apple (covered with dilettante chocolate,
caramel and pecans), gift club
COMMENTS   *Because the proceeds of every item from The Children's Gift
Catalog go to the Children's Home Society and to benefit children and their
families, this is a gift of some very nice products (I actually like the salmon
best) that will give twice.*

China Ranch Date Farm
#8 China Ranch Road
Tecopa, CA 92389
PHONE (760) 852-4415

SIGNATURE PRODUCT **Dates**

ADDITIONAL PRODUCTS Date bread, date cookies, date muffins, date
nut rolls, nuts, dried fruit

Cushman's
3325 Forest Hill Boulevard
West Palm Beach, FL 33406
PHONE (800) 776-7575; FAX (800) 776-4329
E-MAIL cushman@aol.com

SIGNATURE PRODUCT **Cushman HoneyBell oranges**

NEWEST PRODUCT "A Two Muffin Morning" — Wolferman's muffins
and Cushman oranges and grapefruits with apricot spread and marmalade
ADDITIONAL PRODUCTS Grapefruit, tangerines, gift baskets, keylime
cookies, coconut patties, peaches, pears, mangoes, cherries, nectarines,
tomatoes, apples, plums, yams, cheesecake, nuts, fudge, and fruit club
COMMENTS *Unsampled — but the description of the Cushman HoneyBell,
"Considered by some to be the sweetest, juiciest, most flavorful oranges anywhere," makes me eagerly await January (the only month they're available).*

▨ Daniel Weaver Company
15th Avenue & Weavertown Road, P.O. Box 525
Lebanon, PA 17042
PHONE (800) WEAVERS; FAX (717) 274-6103

▨ Diamond Organics
P.O. Box 2159
Freedom, CA 95019
PHONE (888) ORGANIC; FAX (888) 888-6777
WEB SITE http://www.diamondorganics.com
E-MAIL Organics@diamondorganics.com

Farm2You

P.O. Box 9146
Chico, CA 95927
PHONE (888) FARM2YOU; FAX (916) 865-4929
WEB SITE http://www.farm2you.com
E-MAIL steve@farm2you.com

Ferris Valley Groves

P.O. Box 530567
Harlingen, TX 78553-0567
PHONE (800) 748-7182; FAX (210) 412-6148
E-MAIL sarah@valleygroves.com

SIGNATURE PRODUCT **Texas Rio Red Grapefruit**

NEWEST PRODUCT Jalapeno peanut brittle
ADDITIONAL PRODUCTS Navel oranges, homemade Texas brittle
COMMENTS *The fruit was not in season for testing but I tasted the peanut brittle. The regular brittle was great, the jalapeno brittle wasn't bad although it was a little odd eating green brittle. Liked the onion and pepper dressing.*

A Fine Nuthouse: Nuts4u

Nuts & Fruits & Gifts
P.O. Box 1864
Sugar Land, TX 77487
PHONE (800) 688-Nuts4u2 (688-7482); FAX (281) 242-2794
WEB SITE http://www.nuts4u.com
E-MAIL nuts4u@nuts4u.com

Florida Fruit Shippers

5006 Gulfport Boulevard S
Gulfport, FL 33707
PHONE (800) 715-8279; FAX (813) 323-5412
WEB SITE www.orangesonline.com
E-MAIL ffs@orangesonline

SIGNATURE PRODUCT **Grove-fresh Florida oranges and grapefruit**

NEWEST PRODUCT Gourmet food baskets

ADDITIONAL PRODUCTS   Deluxe gift baskets, tropical fruit, vidalia sweet onions, sun-ripened tomatoes, gift fruit calendar collection fruit club, — customer "Thank you" program for businesses

Four Apostles' Ranch
80-700 Avenue 38
Bermuda Dunes, CA 92203
PHONE (619) 345-6171; FAX (619) 345-8901
WEB SITE   www.aureus.com/dates
E-MAIL   brad@aureus.com

SIGNATURE PRODUCT   *Certified Organic Medjool Dates*

Frieda's Inc.
4465 Corporate Center Drive
Los Alamitos, CA 90720
PHONE (800) 241-1771; FAX (714) 816-0273
WEB SITE   www.friedas.com
E-MAIL   mail@friedas.com

Great Food Online
2030 1st Avenue, 3rd Floor
Seattle, WA 98121
PHONE (800) 841-5984; FAX (206) 443-3314
WEB SITE   http://www.greatfood.com
E-MAIL   proprietor@greatfood.com

Hadley Fruit Orchards
50130 Main Street, P.O. Box 246
Cabazon, CA 92230
PHONE (800) 854-5655; FAX (909) 849-8580
E-MAIL   hadley31@aol.com

SIGNATURE PRODUCT   *Dried fruit gift baskets*

ADDITIONAL PRODUCTS   All kinds of dried fruit and gift baskets
COMMENTS   *Great dates!*

Harry and David

2518 S. Pacific Highway, P.O. Box 712
Medford, OR 97501
PHONE (800) 547-3033; FAX (800) 648-6640
WEB SITE   www.harryanddavid.com

SIGNATURE PRODUCT   *Royal Riviera Pears/Fruit-of-the-Month Club*

ADDITIONAL PRODUCTS   Complete line of gourmet fruit and food
products
COMMENTS   *Harry and David are famous for their superior fresh produce.
And with good reason, they are consistently able to provide a good, well-
packaged product. Their pears will always be my favorite and these are on
the "must try" list.*

Knollwood Groves

8053 Lawrence Road
Boynton Beach, FL 33436-1699
PHONE (800) 222-9696; FAX (561) 737-6700

SIGNATURE PRODUCT   *Citrus*

ADDITIONAL PRODUCTS   Oranges, grapefruits, citrus candy, jams and
relishes, salad dressings, dried fruit, tomatoes, onions, avacado, cakes,
flowers, citrus spray and gift baskets
COMMENTS   *It was (unfortunately) the wrong season to sample any of their
fresh produce; but the vidalia dressing was very good!*

Mack's Groves

1180 North Federal Highway
Pompano Beach, FL 33062
PHONE (800) 327-3525; FAX (954) 942-1463
WEB SITE   www.webpc.com/macks/; E-MAIL   macks@gate.net

SIGNATURE PRODUCT   *Honey Bell Tangelos*

NEWEST PRODUCT   Key Lime Cooler Cookies
ADDITIONAL PRODUCTS   Seedless naval oranges, temples, valencia,
pink seedless grapefruit, Florida #1 fancy tomatoes, natural dried fruit

and candies. Also: honey, conch chowder, soft-shelled pecans, jellies and marmalades

COMMENTS   *We nearly fought over who got to eat the last crumbs from the Key Lime Cooler Cookies! Yes, they should be on the "must try" list.*

Manhattan Fruitier

105 East 29th Street
New York, NY 10016
PHONE (800) 841-5718; FAX (212) 689-0479
WEB SITE   www.nystyle.com/manfruit
E-MAIL   manfruit@nystyle.com

Mixon Fruit Farms Inc.

2712 26th Avenue E
Bradenton, FL 34208
PHONE (800) 608-2525; FAX (941) 748-1085
WEB SITE   www.mixon.com
E-MAIL   Info@mixon.com

SIGNATURE PRODUCT   **Fresh Citrus — Oranges & Grapefruit**

NEWEST PRODUCT   Homemade Fudge Salad Dressings
ADDITIONAL PRODUCTS   Citrus candies, jelly & marmalade

Naturally Nuts & Fruity Too!

21661 Avenue 296
Execter, CA 93221
PHONE (209) 477-9569
WEB SITE   http://members.aol.com/nnuts/nnuts.htm
E-MAIL   nnuts@aol.com

ORE-ASIA

4651 NE Riverside Drive
McMinnville, OR 97128
PHONE (503) 434-9766; FAX (503) 434-2809
WEB SITE   www.ore-asia.com
E-MAIL   info@ore-asia.com

SIGNATURE PRODUCT   *Oregon-grown Asian pears*

NEWEST PRODUCT   Oregon-grown Gala apples
ADDITIONAL PRODUCTS   Oregon products: roasted hazelnuts, English toffee, dried Asian pears, hazelnut brittle

Pezzini Farms
460 Nashua Road, P.O. Box 1276
Castroville, CA 95012
PHONE (800) 347-6118; FAX (408) 757-4476
WEB SITE   www.pezzinifarms.com
E-MAIL   artichoke@pezzinifarms.com

R.L. Pearson & Sons
P.O. Box 1892
Winter Haven, FL 33883-1892
PHONE (888) 438-3565
WEB SITE   www.juiceking.com; E-MAIL info@juiceking.com

SIGNATURE PRODUCT   *Citrus*

ADDITIONAL PRODUCTS   Oranges and grapefruits, mangos, avacados, marmalades, fruit club and gift baskets
COMMENTS   *Very nice fresh oranges and grapefruits!*

Seyco Fine Foods
970 E Santa Clara Street
Ventura, CA 93001-3033
PHONE (800) 423-2942; FAX (805) 641-9919
WEB SITE   http://www.west.net/~adunstan/
E-MAIL   adunstan@west.net

Shawnee Canning Co.

212 Cross Junction Road, P.O. Box 657
Cross Junction, VA 22625
PHONE (800) 713-1414; FAX (540) 888-7963
WEB SITE   www.w3ic.com/shawnee/
E-MAIL   shawcan@crosslink.net

SIGNATURE PRODUCT   *Apple, peach, and pumpkin butter*

NEWEST PRODUCT   Pear butter
ADDITIONAL PRODUCTS   Apple sauce, apple syrup, ciders, fresh
   apple, pickles, relish, preserves, jelly, juice-sweetened spreads, salsa,
   barbecue sauce, honey, dressings
COMMENTS   *When you do a project like this book you begin to think all pre-*
   serves and many sauces and condiments taste rather alike; then comes along
   Shawnee. Very good, especially liked the black raspberry preserves. On the
   "must try" list.

Sphinx Date Ranch

3039 N. Scottsdale Road
Scottsdale, AZ 85251
PHONE (800) 482-3283; FAX (602) 941-1840
WEB SITE   calzona.com/sphinx; E-MAIL   sphinx@infinet.rs.com

SIGNATURE PRODUCT   *Medjool dates*

NEWEST PRODUCT   Fruit/gift baskets
ADDITIONAL PRODUCTS   Large variety of dates, date products, dried
   fruit, nuts, jellies, all Arizona products
COMMENTS   *Absolutely wonderful dates.*

Sultan's Delight

P.O. Box 090302
Brooklyn, NY 11209
PHONE (800) 852-5046; FAX (718) 745-2563

Sweet Energy

4 Acorn Lane
Colchester, VT 05446
PHONE (800) 979-3380; FAX (802) 655-1372

SIGNATURE PRODUCT   *Dried apricots*

NEWEST PRODUCT   Apple cranberry apricot rolls
ADDITIONAL PRODUCTS   Figs, dates, giant raisins, homemade apricot
   granola, fancy nuts, the world's best chocolate malt balls, Vermont

cheddar cheese; dried cherries, cranberries, nectarines, peaches, pears, pineapple, prunes and gift boxes

▨ Timber Crest Farms
4791 Dry Creek Road
Healdsburg, CA 95448
PHONE (707) 433-8251; FAX (707) 433-8255
WEB SITE www.timbercrest.com/tcf/
E-MAIL tcf@timbercrest.com

▨ Veggie Express
P.O. Box 29
Sycamore, GA 31790
PHONE (888) 834-4439 or 888-veggiex; FAX (912) 387-6606
WEB SITE www.veggieexpress.com
E-MAIL info@veggieexpress.com

▨ Yasmin Gourmet Food
56 Pleasant Street
Greenville, RI 02828-1920
PHONE (401) 949-2121; FAX (401) 949-0991
WEB SITE hudson.idt.net/~brbina19/
E-MAIL bobbybina@hotmail.com

GIFT BASKETS

A wide range of different products, gourmet grocery stores and gift basket producers.

Alex Patout's Louisiana Foods
221 Royal Street
New Orleans, LA 70130
PHONE (504)525-7788; FAX (504)525-7809
WEB SITE patout.com
E-MAIL patout.com

American Spoon Foods, Inc.
1668 Clarion Avenue, P.O. Box 566
Petoskey, MI 49770
PHONE (800) 222-5886; FAX (616) 347-2512
WEB SITE www.spoon.com
E-MAIL information@spoon.com

Balducci's
11-02 Queens Plaza South
Long Island City, NY 11101
PHONE (800) 225-3822; FAX (718) 786-4125
WEB SITE www.balducci.com

SIGNATURE PRODUCT **Oven-ready beef Wellington**

NEWEST PRODUCT Oven-ready marinated prime-beef
ADDITIONAL PRODUCTS Prosciutto, cheese, breads, smoked fish, caviar, froie gras, pastas and sauces, soups, steak sampler, lobster pot, low-fat ostrich meat, Belgian beef, balsamic vinegars, gift baskets, desserts, sorbets, olive oils, antipasto, salami, sausages
CATALOG INFO Balducci's is famous for having the best of every type of food, and the catalog lusciously displays a beautiful feast.

▦ Bandon's Cheese
680 East 2nd, P.O. Box 1668
Bandon, OR 97411
PHONE (800) 548-8961; FAX (541) 347-2012

▦ Bear Kingdom Vineyard
P.O. Box 2316
Little Rock, AR 72203
PHONE (800) 781-1545; FAX (501) 888-1015
WEB SITE bbonline.com/~bbonline/vnd/bearkingdom/index.html
E-MAIL bearkingdom@juno.com

▦ Beer Across America
55 Albrecht Drive
Lake Bluff, IL 60044
PHONE (880) 854-BEER; FAX (847) 604-8821
WEB SITE www.beeramerica.com

▦ Blood's Hammock Groves
4600 Linton Boulevard
Delray Beach, FL 33445
PHONE (800) 255-5188; FAX (561) 498-0285
WEB SITE www.bhgcitrus.com
E-MAIL blood's@bhgcitrus.com

▦ Boo-Daddy's Chile Pepper Company
P.O. Box 6245
North Augusta, SC 29861-6245
PHONE (800) 436-6794; FAX (706) 790-9898
WEB SITE www.augusta.net/boo_daddy's/
E-MAIL Rkeller@augusta.net

Bountiful Baskets
2117 Concord Pike
Wilmington, DE 19803
PHONE (888) 737-6727; FAX (302) 658-7664
WEB SITE www.coffeecreations.com

SIGNATURE PRODUCT   *Coffee Gift Baskets*

NEWEST PRODUCT   Coffee club
ADDITIONAL PRODUCTS   Teas, pastas in the shape of college mascots,
   fiery foods, candies, snacks
COMMENTS   *The coffees were wonderful. I particularly liked the Sumatra*
   Mandheling.

The Bread Basket L.L.C.

2116 Taft Highway
Signal Mountain, TN 37377
PHONE (800) 581-0339; FAX (423) 886-9332
WEB SITE   http://www.breadbasket.com
E-MAIL   bread@voy.net

SIGNATURE PRODUCT   *Sour Dough*

NEWEST PRODUCT   Happy Cookies
ADDITIONAL PRODUCTS   Cinnamon Breads, cakes, muffins (cream
   cheese). Our primary focus is gift baskets. Shrink wrapped and filled
   with various breads and muffins.
COMMENTS   *Really very nice breads, much like homemade.*

The British Gourmet

45 Wall Street
Madison, CT 06443
PHONE (800) 842-6674; FAX (203) 245-3477
WEB SITE   www.thebritishshoppe.com
E-MAIL   gourmet@thebritisheshoppe.com

Calef's Country Store

Route 9, P.O. Box 57
Barrington, NH 03825
PHONE (603) 664-2231; FAX (603) 664-5857
WEB SITE   www.wertzcandy.com
E-MAIL   wertz@nbn.net

Callaway Gardens
P.O. Box 2000
Pine Mountain, GA 31822-2000
PHONE (800) 280-7524; FAX (706) 663-5058

The Children's Catalog
Children's Home Society of Washington, P.O. Box 15190
Seattle, WA 98115
PHONE (800) 856-5437; FAX (206) 523-1667
WEB SITE   www.chs-wa.org

The Coffee Mug
3405 Sweetwater Road, Suite 434
Lawrenceville, GA 30244
PHONE (770) 446-7138
WEB SITE   www.coffeemug.com

Country Sliced Ham
1321 Guerneville Road
Santa Rosa, CA 95401
PHONE (707) 523-1655
WEB SITE   http://netmar.com/~hamorder
E-MAIL   custom@sonic.net

Cushman's
3325 Forest Hill Boulevard
West Palm Beach, FL 33406
PHONE (800) 776-7575; FAX (800) 776-4329
E-MAIL   cushman@aol.com

Dakin Farm
Route 7, RR1, Box 1775
Ferrisburg, VT 05456
PHONE (800) 993-2546; FAX (802) 425-2765
WEB SITE   www.dakinfarm.com
E-MAIL   dakin@vbimail.champlain.edu

🀫 **Daniel Weaver Company**
15th Avenue & Weavertown Road, P.O. Box 525
Lebanon, PA 17042
PHONE (800) WEAVERS; FAX (717) 274-6103

🀫 **Dessert of the Month**
16805 S. Central Avenue
Carson, CA 90746
PHONE (800) 800-2253; FAX (310) 668-2148

🀫 **DiBruno Bros. House of Cheese**
930 South 9th Street
Philadelphia, PA 19147
PHONE (888) 322-4337; FAX (215) 922-2080
WEB SITE http://www.dibruno.com
E-MAIL dibruno@gim.net

Farmacopia

21900 Summit Road
Los Gatos, CA 95030
PHONE (888) 353-5577; FAX (408) 353-2875
WEB SITE www.farmacopia.com
E-MAIL sbfm@farmacopia.com

SIGNATURE PRODUCT *Gourmet tapenades, canned tuna & salmon*

ADDITIONAL PRODUCTS All of our products are sold at our farmers'
markets in Santa Clara Valley, California. The list includes pistachios,
canned gourmet tuna and salmon, the first U.S. gourmet tapenades,
homemade preserves and toppings, and more

Fine Foods a la Modern

WEB SITE www.finefoods.com
E-MAIL finefoodsa@aol.com

SIGNATURE PRODUCT *Gourmet foods*

ADDITIONAL PRODUCTS We are a collection of products from over a
dozen specialty food producers, each one with their own product line.

Essential Sourcebook: GIFT BASKETS

CATALOG INFO A sample of the various companies' offerings can be seen on our website and can be ordered directly from the company.

Florida Fruit Shippers
5006 Gulfport Boulevard S
Gulfport, FL 33707
PHONE (800) 715-8279; FAX (813) 323-5412
WEB SITE www.orangesonline.com
E-MAIL ffs@orangesonline

Flying Noodle
1 Arrowhead Road
Duxbury, MA 02332
PHONE (800) 566-0599; FAX (617) 934-1527
WEB SITE www.flyingnoodle.com
E-MAIL bigparmesan@flyingnoodle.com

Frieda's Inc.
4465 Corporate Center Drive
Los Alamitos, CA 90720
PHONE (800) 241-1771; FAX (714) 816-0273
WEB SITE www.friedas.com
E-MAIL mail@friedas.com

SIGNATURE PRODUCT **Specialty Produce**

NEWEST PRODUCT Veggibles
ADDITIONAL PRODUCTS Beautiful gift baskets with fresh produce or regional themes (Southwest)

Gazin's
2910 Toulouse Street, P.O. Box 19221
New Orleans, LA 70119-0221
PHONE (800) 262-6410; FAX (504) 827-5319

■ *Gifts from the Illinois Amish Country*
138 S. Vine
Arthur, IL 61911
PHONE (800) 879-2494; FAX (217) 543-2898
WEB SITE www.IllinoisAmishCountry.com/WLPantry/gifthome.htm
E-MAIL AmishCM@net66.com

Great Food Online
2030 1st Avenue, 3rd Floor
Seattle, WA 98121
PHONE (800) 841-5984; FAX (206) 443-3314
WEB SITE http://www.greatfood.com
E-MAIL proprietor@greatfood.com

SIGNATURE PRODUCT **Dried cherries, chocolate decadence tortes**

NEWEST PRODUCT BR Cohn Olive Hill Oil Company premium olive
oils and vinegar sets
ADDITIONAL PRODUCTS Gourmet sausages, smoked hams, turkeys,
quail, jams & jellies, pickled vegetables, coffee beans, herb cheeses
and butters, cheesecakes and brownies, gift baskets, relishes and
sauces, biscotti, dried fruits and berries, and chocolate-covered fruit

■ *Green Mountain Sugar House*
Box 82, Route 100N
Ludlow, VT 05149
PHONE (800) 643-9338; FAX (802) 228-2298
E-MAIL gmsh@ludl.tds.net

■ *Hadley Fruit Orchards*
50130 Main Street, P.O. Box 246
Cabazon, CA 92230
PHONE (800) 854-5655; FAX (909) 849-8580
E-MAIL hadley31@aol.com

Harman's Cheese & Country
1400 Route 117
Sugar Hill, NH 03585
PHONE (603) 823-8000; FAX (603) 823-8000

Harper's Country Hams
2955 US Hwy 51 North, P.O. Box 122
Clinton, KY 42031
PHONE (888) HARPERS; FAX (502) 633-2409
WEB SITE www.hamtastic.com

Harry and David
2518 S. Pacific Highway, P.O. Box 712
Medford, OR 97501
PHONE (800) 547-3033; FAX (800) 648-6640
WEB SITE www.harryanddavid.com

Heaton Pecan Farm
309 Sunrise Boulevard
Clanton, AL 35045
PHONE (800) 446-3531; FAX (205) 755-8677

Heavenly Cheesecakes & Chocolates Inc.
1369 Ridgewood Avenue
Holly Hill, FL 32117
PHONE (904) 673-6670; FAX (904) 673-2367
WEB SITE www.heavenlycheesecakes.com
E-MAIL Heavenlycheesecakes@juno.com

Horizon Foods
Corporate Headquarters
Plainview, NY
PHONE (516) 937-1550
WEB SITE www.horizonfoods.com

How Sweet It Is!

P.O. Box 376
Jenkintown, PA 19046
PHONE (215) 784-9980; FAX (215) 784-0761
WEB SITE   www.howsweet.com
E-MAIL   tomgold@vikingcomputers.com

International Brownie, Inc.

602 Middle Street
Weymouth, MA 02189
PHONE (617) 340-1588; FAX (617) 331-1900
WEB SITE   www.internationalbrownie.com
E-MAIL   brownies@ix.netcom.com

Karen James, Ltd.

896 S. Broadway
Hicksville, NY 11801
PHONE (800) 870-2969; FAX (516) 942-0504
WEB SITE   www.karenjamesltd.com
E-MAIL   karenltd@aol.com

SIGNATURE PRODUCT   *Gift baskets*

NEWEST PRODUCT   Guiseppe's Gourmet Sausage
ADDITIONAL PRODUCTS   Gift baskets: Shore sampler (Bloody Mary
    mix, Virginia peanuts, clams, dip, etc.); A Victorian Tea (teas, key lime
    cookies, etc.); A Feast of the Senses (salsa, tortilla chips, beers, black
    bean dip, etc.); also baskets with non-food items as well

Knollwood Groves

8053 Lawrence Road
Boynton Beach, FL 33436-1699
PHONE (800) 222-9696; FAX (561) 737-6700

Krua Thai

1106 Littlepage Street
Fredericksburg, VA 22401
PHONE (540) 374-9362; FAX (540) 374-9362
WEB SITE   http://www.thaitar.com; E-MAIL   kruathai@thaitara.com

Lambs Farm ⊓ ❀

P.O. Box 520
Libertyville, IL 60048
PHONE (800) 52-LAMBS; FAX (847) 362-6319

SIGNATURE PRODUCT *Butter cookies and preserves*

NEWEST PRODUCT Peanut butter and cashew butter
ADDITIONAL PRODUCTS Gift baskets, greeting cards, hand-dipped
  chocolates, vegetable salsa, fresh baked breads and cakes, dog and cat
  treats and more
COMMENTS *Lambs Farm products are produced by mental handicapped
  adults and are very tasty. I especially liked the salsa and the butter cookies
  (although I prefer my butter cookies without sprinkles). A gift that gives twice.*

▦ Liquor By Wire

2835 N. Sheffield, Suite 409
Chicago, IL 60657
PHONE (800) 621-5150; FAX (773) 325-9576
WEB SITE www.lbw.com;   E-MAIL   lbw2835@aol.com

▦ Manganaro Foods

488 Ninth Avenue
New York, NY 10018
PHONE (800) 4-SALAMI; FAX (212) 239-8355

Manhattan Fruitier

105 East 29th Street
New York, NY 10016
PHONE (800) 841-5718; FAX (212) 689-0479
WEB SITE www.nystyle.com/manfruit; E-MAIL manfruit@nystyle.com

SIGNATURE PRODUCT *Fresh fruit baskets*

ADDITIONAL PRODUCTS Dried fruit, cranberry, ginger, coconut, biscotti, handmade chocolates
CATALOG INFO Stunning presentation; very sophisticated and inviting
  displays of fruit and other lovely food items in baskets and other elegant containers

Maurice's Gourmet Barbeque
1600 Charleston Highway, P.O. Box 6847
West Columbia, SC 29171
PHONE (803) 791-5887; FAX (803) 791-8707
WEB SITE http://www.mauricesbbq.com
E-MAIL maurices@netside.com

Mrs. Beasley's Muffin & Gift Baskets

255 1/2 S. Beverly Drive
Beverly Hills, CA 90746
PHONE (800) MUFFIN1; FAX (310) 668-2148

SIGNATURE PRODUCT *Gift baskets*

ADDITIONAL PRODUCTS   All kinds of muffins and sweet breads plus
tea-cakes and bars in attractive baskets or boxes
COMMENTS *Lovely baked goods, especially liked the lemon cake.*

Only Gourmet

P.O. Box 2214
Orinda, CA 94563
PHONE (888) 413-6637; FAX (510) 531-4981
WEB SITE http://www.onlygourmet.com
E-MAIL alank@onlygourmet.com

SIGNATURE PRODUCT *Coffee Club of the Month — Oren's, Coffee
Roasters of Charleston, Distant Lands Coffee Roaster*

NEWEST PRODUCT   Dilettante Chocolates
ADDITIONAL PRODUCTS   Chocolate truffles, chocolate-covered Queen
Anne cherries, toffee and more from Dilettante Chocolates; hot sauces
from Busteloís Backyard; Jo Bís Hot Sauces; specialty coffees, salad
dressings, capers, olive oils, pasta, balsamic vinegar, and more
COMMENTS *I sampled three products from Only Gourmet: tea, coffee
(marked Rebecca's coffee!) and syrup. All were exceptional and clearly Only
Gourmet is just that. This company is on my "must try" list.*

Palate Partners

2013 Penn Avenue
Pittsburgh, PA 15222
PHONE (800) 565-2816; FAX (412) 642-2822
WEB SITE   http://www.eat-and-drink.com
E-MAIL   shop@eat-and-drink.com

SIGNATURE PRODUCT   *Monthly selection of themed packages*

The Pasta Basket

P.O. Box 176
West Chester, OH 45071
PHONE (800) 759-8706; FAX (513) 777-8422
WEB SITE   www.pastabasket.com

SIGNATURE PRODUCT   *The Pasta Basket*

ADDITIONAL PRODUCTS   The Basket includes the primary ingredients
    to create two delicious pasta dishes, each recipe serves four. Also avail-
    able is The Crate, The Package, The Club and lots of Italian recipes.
COMMENTS   *Very clever idea and the Italian ingedients are very nice.*
    Unusual and fun as a gift for someone else . . . or as a treat for yourself.

Pasta Just For You By Sue

111 West Main
West Dundee, IL 60118
PHONE (800) PASTA-US; FAX (847) 836-1014

The Peanut Patch Inc.

27478 Southampton Parkway, P.O. Box 186
Courtland, VA 23837
PHONE (800) 544-0896; FAX (757) 653-9530
WEB SITE   www.peanutpatch.com
E-MAIL   peanutpatch@gc.net

▨ Pezzini Farms
460 Nashua Road, P.O. Box 1276
Castroville, CA 95012
PHONE (800) 347-6118; FAX (408) 757-4476
WEB SITE www.pezzinifarms.com
E-MAIL artichoke@pezzinifarms.com

▨ The Popcorn Factory
13970 W. Laurel Drive
Lake Forest, IL 60045
PHONE (800) 541-2676; FAX (309) 689-3885
WEB SITE www.popcornfactory.com

▨ R.L. Pearson & Sons
P.O. Box 1892
Winter Haven, FL 33883-1892
PHONE (888) 438-3565
WEB SITE www.juiceking.com
E-MAIL info@juiceking.com

▨ Rowena's
758 West 22nd Street
Norfolk, VA 23517
PHONE (800) 627-8699; FAX (804) 627-1505
WEB SITE pilotonline.com/Rowena's
E-MAIL Rowena's@aol.com

▨ Sam's Wines & Spirits
1720 N. Macey Street
Chicago, IL 60614
PHONE (800) 777-9137; FAX (312) 664-7037
WEB SITE www.sams.wine.com

SENDABASKET — Hoffman's Gift Basket Services
180 Seventh Street
Garden City, NY 11530
PHONE (888) 736-3222; FAX (516) 747- 3680
WEB SITE www.sendabasket.com; E-MAIL bab@sendabasket

SIGNATURE PRODUCT   *The Gourmet Delight*

NEWEST PRODUCT   The Golf Shoe Bag of Goodies

Special Delivery

3820 Ohio Avenue, Suite 4
St. Charles, IL 60174
PHONE (800) 805-GIFT
WEB SITE   www.specialgift.com

SIGNATURE PRODUCT   *Premier gift products*

ADDITIONAL PRODUCTS   Monthly club programs for wine, beer and
    cigars plus two gift packs; the Fine Wine Sampler and the Ultimate
    martini kit
COMMENTS   *Particularly liked the Wit Ale, good flavor and yet not over pow-
    ering as some ales can be. Also liked the cigars but I'm not supposed to com-
    ment on anything but the food.*

Sugarbush

1677 West Lane, Avenue M13
Columbus, OH 43221
PHONE (800) 837-2929; FAX (614) 262-1543
WEB SITE   www.sb-gourmet.com

SIGNATURE PRODUCT   *Gourmet gift baskets*

ADDITIONAL PRODUCTS   Exquisite gift baskets: Picnic baskets that
    include Perrier-Joet champagne, Effie Marie's cookies, Rio Claro Estate
    coffee and 12 more elegant items; wooden crates of black bean dip,
    cheeses, tortilla soup, jelly beans and more. Very creative baskets.
CATALOG INFO   Luscious and inviting catalog

Sutton Place Gourmet

10323 Old Georgetown Road
Bethesda, MD 20814
PHONE (800) 346-8763; FAX (301) 564-3016
WEB SITE   www.suttongourmet
E-MAIL   concierge@suttongourmet.com

SIGNATURE PRODUCT *Quality, creative gift baskets*

ADDITIONAL PRODUCTS Sweet treats, signature collection of exclusive Sutton products, Hay Day breakfast sampler, New England breakfast tea in a wooden crate

CATALOG INFO Lovely catalog with some great looking and unusual gift baskets

Sweet Energy
4 Acorn Lane
Colchester, VT 05446
PHONE (800) 979-3380; FAX (802) 655-1372

TECAPP srl
Lungotevere Flaminio 46
Rome ITALY 196
PHONE ++396/321.51.15;   FAX ++396/321.51.15
WEB SITE   http://www.italiantidbits.com
E-MAIL   e.romano@agora.stm.it

Twin Peaks Gourmet Trading Post

725 Burnett Avenue #6
San Francisco, CA 94131
PHONE (888) 4TPEAKS (487-3257); FAX (415) 824-7849
WEB SITE   http://tpeaks.com
E-MAIL   gourmet@tpeaks.com

SIGNATURE PRODUCT *A full line of gourmet food products*

ADDITIONAL PRODUCTS We carry over 200 products! Olive oils, mustards, hot sauces, BBQ sauce, cheesecake, spices, teas, lobster, pickled vegetables and more

COMMENTS *All of the products I sampled from Twin Peaks were terrific, but I really liked the cheese straws . . . a delightful snack.*

HERBS & SPICES

Fresh herbs, dried herbs and spices, rubs and season packets.

Alex Patout's Louisiana Foods
221 Royal Street
New Orleans, LA 70130
PHONE (504)525-7788; FAX (504)525-7809
WEB SITE patout.com
E-MAIL patout.com

The Barbecue Source
8355 Riverbirch Drive
Roswell, GA 30076
PHONE (888) 252-7686; FAX (770) 552-0462
WEB SITE www.bbqsource.com
E-MAIL don@bbqsource

Big Dave's

765 Quigley Road
Kelowna, British Columba CANADA V1X 1A6
PHONE (250) 762-6867; FAX (250) 862-5828
WEB SITE www.geton.com/bdss
E-MAIL Dave_Abrahamse@bc.sympatico.ca

SIGNATURE PRODUCT **Spice packets/recipe for salsa**

ADDITIONAL PRODUCTS Recipes/spice packets
COMMENTS *These little spice packets are terrific. They really opened my eyes to how nice really fresh homemade salsa can be. Make it in quantity and put your own label on the jar; give it as a gift and everyone will think you're a great cook! Thanks, Dave!*

Classic Kansas City Barbeque Sauces
6105 Manning
Raytown, MO 64133
PHONE (816) 356-9278
WEB SITE http://worldmall.com/bbq/bbq.htm
E-MAIL bbq@worldmall.com

Cosmopolitan Foods
138 Essex Avenue
Glen Ridge, NJ 07042
PHONE (201) 680-4560
WEB SITE www.hotchilisauce.com; E-MAIL hotchilisauce@juno.com

SIGNATURE PRODUCT *Once Tasted Always Wanted*

NEWEST PRODUCT I am on fire: Going to Hell; Holy Sh!t
ADDITIONAL PRODUCTS Indonesian sambals, curry powders, powdered chili pepper, hot sauces, salsas, chili pastes, etc.

Coyote Moon
1709 South Braddick Avenue
Pittsburgh, PA 15218
PHONE (412) 594-4830; FA (412) 242-8710
WEB SITE spicyhot.com/coyotemoon/
E-MAIL coyote@spicyhot.com

Ethnic Tastes
470 Tripp Drive
Golden, CO 80401
PHONE (303) 271-0775; FAX (303) 271-0775
WEB SITE http://www.ethnic-tastes.com
E-MAIL mmisra@ethnic-tastes.com

Farmers Pick Specialty Garlic
10400 Overland Road #393
Boise, ID 83709
PHONE (208) 333-0066
WEB SITE http://www.farmerspick.com
E-MAIL paul@farmerspick.com

▦ The Garlic Survival Company
1094-A1 Revere Avenue
San Francisco, CA 94124
PHONE (800) 3GARLIC; FAX (415) 822-6224

Good Home Cooking Products

🍴

1906-B 1st Avenue North
Irondale, AL 35210
PHONE (205) 951-1928; FAX (205) 956-1817
WEB SITE www.snsnet.net/whistle
E-MAIL whistle@snsnet.net

SIGNATURE PRODUCT *Fried Green Tomato Batter*

NEWEST PRODUCT Original Whistlestop Cafe Cookbook
ADDITIONAL PRODUCTS Caboose Cobbler mix, chicken and seafood
batter, hats, cups, and shirts
COMMENTS *All four of these seasoning products are really very good. I gener-
ally don't have any reason to use shake mixes, but these have given me one.
They produce great chicken, fish, cobbler and, of course, fried green tomatoes!*

▦ The Gourmet Trading Company
1071 Avenida Acaso
Camarillo, CA 93012
PHONE (800) 888-3484; FAX (805) 389-4790
WEB SITE www.gourmettrader.com
E-MAIL trader@gourmettrader.com

▦ The Great Southern Sauce Company
5705 Kavanaugh
Little Rock, AR 72207
PHONE (800) 437-2823; FAX (501) 663-0956
WEB SITE www.greatsauce.com

Hosgood's Company

P.O. Box 1265
Strafford, TX 77497-1265
PHONE (800) 4-GARLIC
WEB SITE www.4garlic.com

SIGNATURE PRODUCT *Garlic seasonings*

ADDITIONAL PRODUCTS All varieties of snacking garlic, from garlic
    with jalapenos to garlic with capers; plus garlic pasta, garlic-flavored
    olive oil, garlic sprinkles, cookbooks, recipes, gift baskets and garlic
    paraphernalia
COMMENTS *The garlic sprinkles were terrific on toast with a little olive oil.*

House Of Fire

1108 Spruce Street
Boulder, CO 80302
PHONE (800) 717-5787; FAX (303) 447-8685
WEB SITE www.houseoffire.com
E-MAIL info@houseoffire.com

Jane Butel's Pecos Valley Spice

2429 Monroe Street, N.E.
Albuquerque, NM 87110
PHONE (800) 473-TACO; FAX (505) 888-4269

Kitchen Secrets

P.O. Box 151467
Dallas, TX 75315
PHONE (800) 527-1311

SIGNATURE PRODUCT *Summer sausage mix*

ADDITIONAL PRODUCTS Salami mix, pepperoni mix, bologna mix,
    chili mix
COMMENTS *These little packets of seasoning mix are very nice, a good addi-
    tion to venison, meat loaf, particularly if your guests are unfamiliar with game.*

▦ Konriko
307 Ann Street, P.O. Box 10640
New Iberia, LA 70560
PHONE (800) 551-3245; FAX (318) 365-5806

▦ Louisiana French Market Online
4614 Tupello Street
Baton Rouge, LA 70808
PHONE (504) 928-1428; FAX (504) 774-4085
WEB SITE http://www.louisianafrenchmarket.com
E-MAIL service@louisianafrenchmarket.com

▦ Magic Seasonings
New Orleans, LA 70123
PHONE (800) 457-2857; FAX (501) 731-3579
WEB SITE www.chefpaul.com
E-MAIL info@chefpaul.com

▦ The Oriental Pantry
423 Great Road
Acton, MA 01720
PHONE (800) 828-0368; FAX (617) 275-4506
WEB SITE www.orientalpantry.com
E-MAIL oriental@orientalpantry.com

▦ Panola Pepper Corp.
Route 2, Box 148
Lake Providence, LA 71254
PHONE (800) 256-3013; FAX (318) 559-3003
WEB SITE www.southernnet.com/panola_peppers

▦ Pueblo Harvest Foods
San Juan Agriculture Cooperative, P.O. Box 1188
San Juan Pueblo, NM 87566
PHONE (888) 511-1120; FAX (505) 747-3148
WEB SITE www.puebloharvest.com
E-MAIL puebloharv@aol.com

Sam McGees Hot Gourmet
8995 Finucane
Hayden, ID 83835
PHONE (208) 762-2627
WEB SITE http://sammcgees.com
E-MAIL troxel@nidlink.com

San Francisco Herb Co.

250 14th Street
San Francisco, CA 94103
PHONE (800) 227-4530; FAX (415) 861-4440
WEB SITE www.sfherb.com
E-MAIL neil@sfherb.com

SIGNATURE PRODUCT **Dried herbs**

NEWEST PRODUCT Pink peppercorns
ADDITIONAL PRODUCTS Over 400 items are available. Spices, teas,
herbs and potpourri ingredients in 4 oz. and 1 pound bags
COMMENTS *Lovely fat juniper berries and very flavorful thyme. The price is
such that it makes giving away herbs an everyday event.*

Sierra Sunset
P.O. Box 525
Crugars, NY 10521
PHONE (800) 832-8990; FAX (914) 739-7541

Spice Merchant
P.O. Box 524
Jackson Hole, WY 83001
PHONE (800) 551-5999; FAX (307) 733-6343
WEB SITE emall.com/spke
E-MAIL 71553.436@compuserve.con

Tree Mouse Edibles Inc.

RR 4 Site 430 C32
Courtenay, British Columbia CANADA V9N-7J3
PHONE (250) 337-5518; FAX (250) 337-5682
WEB SITE   www.vquest.com/treemouse
E-MAIL   tremouse@comox.island.net

SIGNATURE PRODUCT   *Mulling Spices*

NEWEST PRODUCT   Bottled Bread Mixes
ADDITIONAL PRODUCTS   Pepper mill blends; several dry seasonings
     for cooking (no salt, no MSG); gourmet mustards; fruit and herb wine
     vinegars; beer and wine breads; rose petal jelly, marmalade; assorted
     gift packs
COMMENTS   *Very nice seasonings. The peppercorns are a good size; not too
     big, not too little.*

MEALS

Entire meals, freeze dried, packaged or frozen.

AlpineAire Foods

P.O. Box 926
Nevada City, CA 95959
PHONE (800) FAB-MEAL; FAX (916) 272-2624

SIGNATURE PRODUCT **Pouch food for outdoor gourmets**

ADDITIONAL PRODUCTS Complete dehydrated menu items that
require little or no cooking for backpackers and other outdoor enthusi-
asts. Foods include: entrees of seafood, meatless, chicken, turkey, beef;
side dishes, soups, breakfast foods, fruits, desserts, beverages and more
COMMENTS *These meals in a pouch were really very good. Definitely worth
taking on a backpacking trip or to keep on hand for a quick, filling lunch.*

Cibolo Junction Food & Spice Company Inc.

3013 Aztec Road NE
Albuquerque, NM 87107
PHONE (800) 683-9628; FAX (505) 888-1972
WEB SITE www.cibolojunction.com
E-MAIL info@cibolojunction.com

Diane's Gourmet Luxuries

11121 N. Rodney Parhan
Little Rock, AR 72212
PHONE (501) 224-2639; FAX (501) 224-8921
WEB SITE www.dianes-gourmet.com
E-MAIL diane@diane-gourmet.com

SIGNATURE PRODUCT **Ready-to-serve food**

ADDITIONAL PRODUCTS Full dinners with main course, salad, bread
and desserts. Casseroles include everything from chicken pot pie,

chicken enchiladas, lasagna to jambalaya and elegant shrimp casserole (casseroles can be purchased by themselves)

Ethnic Tastes
470 Tripp Drive
Golden, CO 80401
PHONE   (303) 271-0775;   FAX   (303) 271-0775
WEB SITE   http://www.ethnic-tastes.com
E-MAIL   mmisra@ethnic-tastes.com

Flying Fajitas
13710 Chittim Oak
San Antonio, TX 78232
PHONE (800) 290-3411
WEB SITE   www.fajitas.com
E-MAIL   Flyingfajitas@stic.net

Maurice's Gourmet Barbeque
1600 Charleston Highway, P.O. Box 6847
West Columbia, SC 29171
PHONE (803) 791-5887; FAX (803) 791-8707
WEB SITE   http://www.mauricesbbq.com
E-MAIL   maurices@netside.com

Philly Food Division of Dial-A-Party Catering
107 S. Monroe Street
Media, PA 19063
PHONE (610) 565-4386; FAX (610) 566-8200
WEB SITE   http://www.phillypretzels.com
E-MAIL   philly@inet.net

Pueblo Harvest Foods
San Juan Agriculture Cooperative, P.O. Box 1188
San Juan Pueblo, NM 87566
PHONE (888) 511-1120; FAX (505) 747-3148
WEB SITE   www.puebloharvest.com
E-MAIL   puebloharv@aol.com
SIGNATURE PRODUCT   *Dried Green Chile Stew*

NEWEST PRODUCT   Three Sisters Stew
ADDITIONAL PRODUCTs   Quick-cooking Posole Stew, Spicy Black
    Bean Soup, Smoky Corn & Tomato Soup, Smoked Dried Tomatoes,
    Whole Dried Green Chile, Dried Melons

Superbly Southwestern
2400 Rio Grande NW #1-171
Albuquerque, NM 87104
PHONE (800) 467-4HOT
WEB SITE   www.hotchile.com
E-MAIL   hotchile@aol.com

MEATS

Beef, pork and poultry; also buffalo, venisons and smoked meats.

Alaska Sausage & Seafood

2914 Artic Boulevard, P.O. Box 92157
Anchorage, AK 99503-2157
PHONE (907) 562-3636; FAX (907) 562-7343
WEB SITE   www.alaskanet.com
E-MAIL   aks@alaska.net

SIGNATURE PRODUCT   **Reindeer Sausage**

NEWEST PRODUCT   Turkey Pastrami
ADDITIONAL PRODUCTS   Specializing in a variety of sausages made
    with reindeer meat; also smoked salmon, German sausages, imported
    spreads and cheeses and gift packages
COMMENTS   *Very nice reindeer sausage, both the hot and the regular were tasty.*

Alaskan Gourmet Seafoods

1020 West International Airport Road, P.O. Box 190733
Anchorage, AK 99519
PHONE (800) 288-3740; FAX (907) 563-2592
WEB SITE   alaska.net/~akfoods
E-MAIL   akfoods@alaska.net

Alex Patout's Louisiana Foods

221 Royal Street
New Orleans, LA 70130
PHONE (504)525-7788; FAX (504)525-7809
WEB SITE   patout.com
E-MAIL   patout.com

Allen Brothers — The Great Steakhouse Steaks™

3737 S. Halsted Street
Chicago, IL 60609
PHONE (800) 957-0111; FAX (800) 890-9146
WEB SITE http://www.allenbrothers.com
E-MAIL info@allenbrothers.com

SIGNATURE PRODUCT **USDA Prime aged steaks served at America's finest steakhouses**

ADDITIONAL PRODUCTS We also offer the highest quality USDA Prime beef roasts as well as veal, lamb, pork, gourmet chicken items, lobster tails and cheesecakes.

COMMENTS *These are exceptional steaks and are definitely on my "must try" list.*

AlpineAire Foods

P.O. Box 926
Nevada City, CA 95959
PHONE (800) FAB-MEAL; FAX (916) 272-2624

Amana Meat Shop & Smokehouse

4513 F Street, P.O. Box 158
Amana, IA 52203
PHONE (800) 373-6328; FAX (800) 3733710
WEB SITE amanameats@www.jeonet.com
E-MAIL amanams@netins.net

SIGNATURE PRODUCT **Amana ham**

ADDITIONAL PRODUCTS Steaks, pork chops, turkey, sausages, cheese, and bacon

Balducci's

11-02 Queens Plaza South
Long Island City, NY 11101
PHONE (800) 225-3822; FAX (718) 786-4125
WEB SITE www.balducci.com

Big Sky Buffalo
South Main Street, P.O. Box 224
Granville, ND 58741
PHONE (800) 570-7220; FAX (701) 728-6505
WEB SITE   http://www.tradecorridor.com/bigskybuffalo
E-MAIL   cnatc@minot.ndak.net

SIGNATURE PRODUCT   *Buffalo Meat Products*

NEWEST PRODUCT   All kinds of new products
ADDITIONAL PRODUCTS   All types of North Dakota grown buffalo meat.

Bunky's Smokehouse Bar-B-Q
201 East Henson
Haines City, FL 33844
PHONE (800) 730-0123
WEB SITE   http://www.coolbiz.com/bunky/

SIGNATURE PRODUCT   *Hams, turkeys*

NEWEST PRODUCT   Home Made Bar-B-Q Sauces

Burger's Ozark Country Cured Ham
Route 3, P.O. Box 3248
California, MO 65018
PHONE (800) 624-5426; FAX (573) 796-3137
WEB SITE   www.smokehouse.com

SIGNATURE PRODUCT   *Country cured ham*

NEWEST PRODUCT   Smoked poultry
ADDITIONAL PRODUCTS   City ham (moist cured), fresh beef steaks,
    buffalo, fresh and cured ribs, cured and smoked pork chops and ten-
    derloin, Canadian bacon, breakfast sausage, summer sausage and
    cheese; country cured bacon and city bacon

Callaway Gardens

P.O. Box 2000
Pine Mountain, GA 31822-2000
PHONE (800) 280-7524; FAX (706) 663-5058

Caviar Delight & Gifts Company

33020 10th Avenue SW, Suite P302
Federal Way, WA 98023
PHONE (800) 572-6180 access code 50; FAX (253) 835-0468
WEB SITE www.caviargift.com; E-MAIL sales@caviargift.com

Country Sliced Ham

1321 Guerneville Road
Santa Rosa, CA 95401
PHONE (707) 523-1655
WEB SITE http://netmar.com/~hamorder
E-MAIL custom@sonic.net

SIGNATURE PRODUCT *Honey Glazed Spiral Sliced Ham*

ADDITIONAL PRODUCTS Gourmet mustards from California's North
Coast, and wonderful gift baskets.

Country Store

R.D. #2 Box P31
Pennsdale, PA 17756
PHONE (800) 313-HAMS; FAX (717) 546-8626
WEB SITE www.sunlink.net/%7Ectrystre
E-MAIL ctrystre@earth.sunlink.net

SIGNATURE PRODUCT *Naturally smoked and cured hams*

NEWEST PRODUCT Spiral smoked and glazed, smoked boneless ham
ADDITIONAL PRODUCTS Smoked ring bologna (plain, hot, garlic);
smoked stick bologna (plain, hot, garlic, cheese); naturally smoked
bacon; smoked sausage; hot dogs; scrapple; dipping mustard
COMMENTS *All of their products are great; but I really liked the naturally
smoked bacon, and the dipping mustard was fantastic.*

Cybertown.net

P.O. Box 5003-121
Carpinteria, CA 93013
PHONE (800) 585-8567
WEB SITE http://www.cybertown.net
E-MAIL food@cybertown.net

SIGNATURE PRODUCT *Sirloin and T-Bone Steaks*

NEWEST PRODUCT Beef Products
ADDITIONAL PRODUCTS In addition to a wide variety of cookbooks
we are in the process of adding a complete selection of meat products
with the addition of exotic meats such as buffalo, venison and emu.

Dakin Farm

Route 7, RR1, Box 1775
Ferrisburg, VT 05456
PHONE (800) 993-2546; FAX (802) 425-2765
WEB SITE www.dakinfarm.com
E-MAIL dakin@vbimail.champlain.edu

SIGNATURE PRODUCT *Cob-smoked, bone-in ham*

NEWEST PRODUCT Black forest hams and turkeys
ADDITIONAL PRODUCTS Pure Vermont, maple syrup, aged Vermont
cheddar cheese, spiral sliced, maple glazed hams, cob-smoked
turkeys, cob-smoked bacon & sausage
COMMENTS *These are wonderful New England products; and the pancake
mix was easy-to-use, had the buttermilk already in it and was very good.*

Daniel Weaver Company

15th Avenue & Weavertown Road, P.O. Box 525
Lebanon, PA 17042
PHONE (800) WEAVERS; FAX (717) 274-6103

SIGNATURE PRODUCT *Smoked bologna*

ADDITIONAL PRODUCTS Hams, bacon, dried beef, turkeys, gift baskets, munchies, dried fruit, fruit spread, dried sweet corn, relish,
shoo-fly pie, chocolates

COMMENTS   *The bacon was the real thing: thick and smokey tasting, very good.*

Dave's Gourmet Inc.
1255 Montgomery Avenue
San Bruno, CA 94066
PHONE (800) 758-0372; FAX (415) 794-0340
WEB SITE   davesgourmet.com
E-MAIL   insanity@davesgourmet.com

Diane's Gourmet Luxuries
11121 N. Rodney Parhan
Little Rock, AR 72212
PHONE (501) 224-2639; FAX (501) 224-8921
WEB SITE   www.dianes-gourmet.com
E-MAIL   diane@diane-gourmet.com

DiBruno Brothers House of Cheese
930 South 9th Street
Philadelphia, PA 19147
PHONE (888) 322-4337; FAX (215) 922-2080
WEB SITE   http://www.dibruno.com
E-MAIL   dibruno@gim.net

Dixie Chili
Newport, KY 41071
PHONE (606) 291-5337 & (606) 291-5337; FAX   (606) 291-5547
WEB SITE   www.dixiechili.com; E-MAIL   dixiechili@fuse.net

SIGNATURE PRODUCT   **Cincinnati-style chili**

COMMENTS   *Not bad on spagetti. Good on a camping trip.*

Dreisbach's Steaks

1135 South Locust Street
Grand Island, NE 68801
PHONE (800) 658-3111; FAX (308) 381-3636
WEB SITE   209.43.39.109/Dreisbach.html
E-MAIL   Dreisbach@cnweb.com

SIGNATURE PRODUCT   *Dry-aged beef*

ADDITIONAL PRODUCTS   All cuts of dry-aged beef, prime rib of beef, porterhouse-style pork chops, surf-and-turf steak and lobster

COMMENTS   *These are extraordinary steaks, absolutely on the "must try" list.*

Farm Pac Kitchens

500 Front Street, P.O. Box 192
Yoakum, TX 77995
PHONE (800) 999-6997; FAX (800) 999-6606
WEB SITE   www.farmpac.com; E-MAIL   gkusak@farmpac.com

SIGNATURE PRODUCT   **Smoked Meats**

NEWEST PRODUCT   Chardonnay Herb Smoked Turkey Breast
ADDITIONAL PRODUCTS   Lemon Peppered Smoked Turkey; Boneless Peppered Ham; Beef Jerky; Smoked Beef Brisket; Spiral Sliced Hams.

CATALOG INFO   Farm Pac is the producer of smoked meats for a dozen or more catalogs which have a private label arrangement with them.

COMMENTS   *The smoked turkey breast was great!*

Foods of New York

66 Peconic Avenue
Medford, NY 11763
PHONE (800) HOTDOG-6; FAX (516) 654-9109
WEB SITE   http://www.nyhotdog.com; E-MAIL steve@nyhotdog.com

Furtado's

544 North Underwood
Fall River, MA 02720
PHONE (800) 845-4800; FAX (508) 679-5999

Great Food Online

2030 1st Avenue, 3rd Floor
Seattle, WA 98121
PHONE (800) 841-5984; FAX (206) 443-3314
WEB SITE http://www.greatfood.com; E-MAIL proprietor@greatfood.com

The Hamlet

9107 S. Sheridan
Tulsa, OK 74133
PHONE (888) 420-HAMS; FAX (918) 495-0843
WEB SITE www.hamlethams.com
E-MAIL sales@hamlethams.com

SIGNATURE PRODUCT *Prime honey glazed, sugar cured, spiral-cut ham*

ADDITIONAL PRODUCTS Turkeys and specialty gourmet food items
and unique gifts
COMMENTS *I loved this ham. A nice sweet, not too salty, ham. Very, very nice.*

Harper's Country Hams

2955 U.S. Highway 51 North, P.O. Box 122
Clinton, KY 42031
PHONE (888) HARPERS; FAX (502) 633-2409
WEB SITE www.hamtastic.com

SIGNATURE PRODUCT *Old-fashioned country ham, bacon, smoked
sausage*

NEWEST PRODUCT Cooked smoked city ham
ADDITIONAL PRODUCTS BBQ ribs, turkey breasts, home-made jams,
gift boxes, country ham jerky, red-eye gravy

Horizon Foods

Corporate Headquarters
Plainview, NY
PHONE (516) 937-1550
WEB SITE www.horizonfoods.com

SIGNATURE PRODUCT *Beef*

ADDITIONAL PRODUCTS Quality cuts of beef, poultry, pork, seafood and
gourmet pizza, pasta and cheesecake ordered from our catalog or website
and delivered from 26 regional suppliers with no shipping charges

Louis Mueller Barbecue

206 W. 2nd Street
Taylor, TX 76574
PHONE (800) 580-6687; FAX (512) 365-6332
WEB SITE www.texasbbq.com
E-MAIL webmaster@texasbbq.com

SIGNATURE PRODUCT *Barbecue; brisket, ribs, sausage*

Manganaro Foods

488 Ninth Avenue
New York, NY 10018
PHONE (800) 4-SALAMI; FAX (212) 239-8355

Maurice's Gourmet Barbeque

1600 Charleston Highway, P.O. Box 6847
West Columbia, SC 29171
PHONE (803) 791-5887; FAX (803) 791-8707
WEB SITE http://www.mauricesbbq.com
E-MAIL maurices@netside.com

Mid-Atlantic Food

280 West Avenue
Long Beach, NJ 07740
PHONE (800) 748-3644; FAX (908) 229-2964
WEB SITE www.virtualfoods.com
E-MAIL pdelgand@mars.superlink.net

SIGNATURE PRODUCT *Boardwalk Griddle Franks*

ADDITIONAL PRODUCTS New Jersey Beefsteak Tomatoes

Montreal Internet Deli & Catering

175 Poplar Road
Montreal, Quebec CANADA H9A 2A6
PHONE (514) 684-5321; FAX (514) 421-0534
WEB SITE http://www.vir.com/~can/bagel/
E-MAIL can@vir.com

New Braunfels Smokehouse

P.O. Box 311159
New Braunfels, TX 78131-1159
PHONE (800) 537-6932; FAX (210) 625-7660

SIGNATURE PRODUCT **Smoked meats**

ADDITIONAL PRODUCTS Smoked brisket, baby baked ribs, smoked
pork & beef sausage, various jerkys and sauces
COMMENTS *Turkey jerky was good and a little different.*

Nordic House

3421 Telegraph Avenue
Oakland, CA 94609
PHONE (800) 854-6435; FAX (510) 653-1936
WEB SITE nordichouse.com
E-MAIL pia@nordichouse.com

Oinkers

1500 E. 7th
Atlantic, IA 50022
PHONE (712) 243-3606; FAX (712) 243-5688
WEB SITE www.neyins.net.\showcaseoinkers

SIGNATURE PRODUCT **Oinker sauce**

NEWEST PRODUCT Oinker burgers (pig-shaped)
COMMENTS *The Oinker sauce is fanfastic, a cut above most BBQ sauces.*

Omaha Steaks

P.O. Box 3300
Omaha, NE 68103
PHONE (800) 228-9055; FAX (402) 597-8222
WEB SITE www.omahasteaks.com
E-MAIL info@omahasteaks.com

SIGNATURE PRODUCT **Steaks**

ADDITIONAL PRODUCTS Seafood, poultry, and other gourmet foods

Seyco Fine Foods

970 E Santa Clara Street
Ventura, CA 93001-3033
PHONE (800) 423-2942; FAX (805) 641-9919
WEB SITE http://www.west.net/~adunstan/
E-MAIL adunstan@west.net

TECAPP srl

Lungotevere Flaminio 46
Rome ITALY 196
PHONE ++396/321.51.15; FAX ++396/321.51.15
WEB SITE http://www.italiantidbits.com; E-MAIL e.romano@agora.stm.it

Usinger's Famous Sausage

1030 North Old World 3rd Street
Milwaukee, WI 53202
PHONE (800) 558-9997; FAX (414) 291-5277

SIGNATURE PRODUCT   *Old-fashioned natural casing weiners*

NEWEST PRODUCT   Fire roasted BBQ beef eye of round
ADDITIONAL PRODUCTS   Fire-roasted BBQ pork loin, braunschweiger,
    all-beef summer sausage and salami, black forest hams, bratwurst,
    Italian sausages
COMMENTS   *I grew up in Chicago believing Usinger's meat products were
    the best. I'm happy that they still are, my favorites are the weiners and the
    braunschweiger.*

Venison America

P.O. Box 86
Rosemount, MN 55068
PHONE (800) 310-2360; FAX (612) 686-7077
WEB SITE www.venisonamerica.com

SIGNATURE PRODUCT   *Smoked venison roast*

NEWEST PRODUCT   Smoked venison roast
ADDITIONAL PRODUCTS   Kippered steak, sticks, jerky, brats, and patties
COMMENTS   *Was sent only jerky to sample but it was good.*

Venison World Inc.

Corner Highway 83 & 87, P.O. Box S
Eden, TX 76837
PHONE (800) 460-5326; FAX (915) 869-7220
E-MAIL   venison@gte.net

SIGNATURE PRODUCT   *Axis Venison*

ADDITIONAL PRODUCTS   Jerky: traditional or spicy; snack sticks, traditional or spicy; 6-pack: summer sausage, traditional or with jalepeno
 & cheese; smoked tenders; dried rings; smoked rings; smoked
 chunks; chili; ground venison; pan sausage; fresh cuts i.e., steaks
COMMENTS   *Very nice venison sausage.*

Virginia Diner

P.O. Box 1030
Wakefield, VA 23888
PHONE (800) 868-6887; FAX (757) 899-2281
WEB SITE   www.vadiner.com
E-MAIL   vadiner@infi.net

HEALTH & ORGANIC FOODS

Organic, low-sodium and san sucre foods, power bars and food supplements.

 1-800-GRANOLA
P.O. Box 756
Amherst, MA 01004
PHONE (800) GRANOLA
WEB SITE www.800granola.com
E-MAIL info@800granola.com

Bandon's Cheese
680 East 2nd, P.O. Box 1668
Bandon, OR 97411
PHONE (800) 548-8961; FAX (541) 347-2012

Barth's Vitamins
3890 Park Central Boulevard, North
Pompano Beach, FL 33064
PHONE (800) 645-2328; FAX (800) 285-8155

SIGNATURE PRODUCT **Barth's brain bar**

NEWEST PRODUCT Barth's citrimix bar
ADDITIONAL PRODUCTS A complete line of health products
COMMENTS *The citrimix bar actually tasted good, and I think it did give me the energy to finish this book.*

Bernard Food Industries
3540 W. Jarvis Avenue
Skokie, IL 60204
PHONE (800) 325-5409; FAX (847) 679-5417
WEB SITE www.diet-shoppe.com

SIGNATURE PRODUCT   *Sweet 'N Low cake and frosting mixes (sugar-free)*

NEWEST PRODUCT   French vanilla and mocha cappuccino mousse mixes
ADDITIONAL PRODUCTS   San sucre mousse mixes, sans sucre sugar-free cinammon sugar
COMMENTS   *The products, which are designed for those folks who crave desserts but can't have sugar, do a good, honest job of making a tasty cookie, cake, or mousse without the sugar.*

Diamond Organics

P.O. Box 2159
Freedom, CA 95019
PHONE (888) ORGANIC; FAX (888) 888-6777
WEB SITE   http://www.diamondorganics.com
E-MAIL   Organics@diamondorganics.com

SIGNATURE PRODUCT   *The Original Organic Fruit & Veggie Sampler*

NEWEST PRODUCT   Diamondbars — totally organic energy bar
ADDITIONAL PRODUCTS   A complete year-round selection of the freshest, best tasting, organically grown fruits, vegetables, flowers & more. Delivered direct to home cooks nationwide. No minimum order, order exactly what you need
COMMENTS   *This produce is extraordinary and is definitely on the "must try" list. Even if you don't want to eat it, just to look at it gives you a lift and a breath of fresh air . . . but do be sure to eat it, too. It's fantastic!*

Easy Exchange — "Snack 15"

Sierra Sunset, P.O. Box 525
Crugars, NY 10521
PHONE (800) 832-8990; FAX (914) 739-7541

SIGNATURE PRODUCT   *Diet-control snacks*

ADDITIONAL PRODUCTS   Fruit & Nut Mix; Chewy Chocolate Cookie Bar
COMMENTS   *These healthy snacks for those who must control their carbohydrate intake taste really good. Honest.*

▦ Golden Choice Foods
Jct. 731 and Riverrun Road, P.O. Box 640
Lancaster, VA 22503
PHONE (800) 988-5181; FAX (804) 462-0131
WEB SITE http:www.hey.net/users/golden
E-MAIL golenchoice@hey.net

▦ The Gourmet Trading Company
1071 Avenida Acaso
Camarillo, CA 93012
PHONE (800) 888-3484; FAX (805) 389-4790
WEB SITE www.gourmettrader.com
E-MAIL trader@gourmettrader.com

▦ Gray's Grist Mill
P.O. Box 422
Adamsville, RI 02801
PHONE (508) 636-6075

▦ Hungry Bear Hemp Foods
P.O. Box 12175
Eugene, OR 97440
PHONE (541) 767-3811; FAX (541) 767-3811
WEB SITE www.efn.org/~gordon_k/Hungrybear.html
E-MAIL eathemp@efn.org

▦ Indiana Botanic Gardens
P.O. Box 5, Department FIIW
Hammond, IN 46325
PHONE (800) 644-8327; FAX (219) 947-4148
WEB SITE www.botanichealth.com
E-MAIL botanichealth@niia.net

▦ Marmix Company
P.O. Box 1458
Newport Beach, CA 92659-0458
PHONE (888) 627-4649; FAX (714) 673-1927
WEB SITE www.marimix.com

Montreal Internet Deli & Catering

175 Poplar Road
Montreal, Quebec CANADA H9A 2A6
PHONE (514) 684-5321; FAX (514) 421-0534
WEB SITE http://www.vir.com/~can/bagel/
E-MAIL can@vir.com

SIGNATURE PRODUCT *Monteral World Famous Bagels*

NEWEST PRODUCT Montreal World Famous Kosher Smoked Meat
ADDITIONAL PRODUCTS Montreal World Famous Kosher Smoked
Turkey

SEAFOOD

Fresh fish from salmon to halibut, plus shellfish, canned and smoked fish and shellfish, and caviar.

Alaskan Gourmet Seafoods

1020 West International Airport Road, P.O. Box 190733
Anchorage, AK 99519
PHONE (800) 288-3740; FAX (907) 563-2592
WEB SITE alaska.net/~akfoods
E-MAIL akfoods@alaska.net

SIGNATURE PRODUCT **Smoked Alaskan salmon**

NEWEST PRODUCT 3 oz. skinless-boneless canned salmon
ADDITIONAL PRODUCTS Complete line of Alaskan food items from reindeer steaks to fresh Alaskan seafood

Alex Patout's Louisiana Foods

221 Royal Street
New Orleans, LA 70130
PHONE (504)525-7788; FAX (504)525-7809
WEB SITE patout.com
E-MAIL patout.com

Allen Brothers — The Great Steakhouse Steaks™

3737 S. Halsted Street
Chicago, IL 60609
PHONE (800) 957-0111; FAX (800) 890-9146
WEB SITE http://www.allenbrothers.com
E-MAIL info@allenbrothers.com

Balducci's
11-02 Queens Plaza South
Long Island City, NY 11101
PHONE (800) 225-3822; FAX (718) 786-4125
WEB SITE www.balducci.com

Caviar Delight & Gifts Company
33020 10th Avenue SW, Suite P302
Federal Way, WA 98023
PHONE (800) 572-6180 access code 50; FAX (253) 835-0468
WEB SITE www.caviargift.com
E-MAIL sales@caviargift.com

SIGNATURE PRODUCT **Caspian Sea Caviar and Smoked Salmon**

ADDITIONAL PRODUCTS Fois gras, pates, olive oil, truffle oil, balsamic vinegar

The Children's Catalog
Children's Home Society of Washington, P.O. Box 15190
Seattle, WA 98115
PHONE (800) 856-5437; FAX (206) 523-1667
WEB SITE www.chs-wa.org

Clambake Celebrations
9 West Road
Orleans, MA 02653
PHONE (800) 423-4038; FAX (508) 255-9610
WEB SITE www.netplaza.com/clambake
E-MAIL clambake@capecod.net

SIGNATURE PRODUCT **Lobster clambake to go**

NEWEST PRODUCT Lobster chowder
ADDITIONAL PRODUCTS New England lobster dinner, lobsters to go, steamers to go, chocolates n' fruit celebration

Collandra, Inc.

2790 NW 104th Court
Miami, FL 33172
PHONE (800) 673-0532; FAX (305) 380-0859
WEB SITE www.caribplace.com/foods/trout.htm
E-MAIL colland@earthlink.net

SIGNATURE PRODUCT **Caribbean food**

ADDITIONAL PRODUCTS Island-style smoked trout, Wallenford Blue
100% Jamaican Blue Mountain Coffee
COMMENTS *The Jamaican coffee was marvelous! And the trout superb.*

The Crab Place

4391 Beechwood Place
Crisfield, MD 21817
PHONE (410) 968-1609
WEB SITE www.crabplace.com; E-MAIL crab@shore.intercom.net

SIGNATURE PRODUCT **Maryland Blue Crabs (hard & soft shell)**

NEWEST PRODUCT Maryland crab cakes
ADDITIONAL PRODUCTS Maryland crab meat

Ducktrap River Fish Farms

RR 2, Box 378
Lincolnville, ME 04849
PHONE (800) 828-3825; FAX (207) 763-4235
WEB SITE ducktrap.com; E-MAIL smoked@ducktrap

SIGNATURE PRODUCT **Kendall Brook Smoked Salmon**

NEWEST PRODUCT Seafood sauces
ADDITIONAL PRODUCTS Many smoked seafood items from smoked
trout to several types of smoked salmon and mussels. Also, pates.
CATALOG INFO Very nice
COMMENTS *The smoked salmons were, of course, good; but I particularly
liked the smoked trout and mussels.*

Dunns Seafare

Jamestown Business Park, Finglas
Dublin, IRELAND 11
PHONE   00-353-1-8643100; FAX 00-353-1-8643109
WEB SITE   www/clubi.ie/dunns-seafare
E-MAIL   dunns@clubi.ie

SIGNATURE PRODUCT   *Smoked Irish wild salmon*

ADDITIONAL PRODUCTS   Smoked Irish farmed salmon

Ekone Oyster Co.

29 Holt Road
South Bend, WA 98586
PHONE (888) 875-5494; FAX (360) 875-6058

SIGNATURE PRODUCT   *Fresh smoked oysters*

NEWEST PRODUCT   Habanero hot smoked oysters
ADDITIONAL PRODUCTS   Fresh packed oysters in various sizes, smoked
   oysters in vacuum-sealed pouches and canned smoked oysters
COMMENTS   *The fresh smoked oysters (vacuum-sealed pouch) were very nice
   (different than canned oysters or fresh); liked the habanero oysters but am a
   little of the mind "Why mess with a great (i.e. plain) taste?"*

Elizabeth Island Lobsters

353 Enterprise Drive
Somerset, MA 02725
PHONE (508) 677-3283
WEB SITE   members.aol.com/eilobsters; E-MAIL eilobsters@aol.com

SIGNATURE PRODUCT   *Fresh New England lobster*

Farmacopia

21900 Summit Road
Los Gatos, CA 95030
PHONE (888) 353-5577; FAX (408) 353-2875
WEB SITE   www.farmacopia.com
E-MAIL   sbfm@farmacopia.com

Fruge Aquafarms

525 E. 8th Street
Crowley, LA 70526
PHONE (888) 254-8626
WEB SITE www.cajuncrawfish.com
E-MAIL cajuncrawfish@worldnet.att.com

SIGNATURE PRODUCT **Live crawfish**

ADDITIONAL PRODUCTS Fresh crawfish tailmeat, seasonings (boiling spices)

Glacier Fresh Seafoods

3 1/2 Seward Highway, P.O. Box 1989
Seward, AK 99664
PHONE (907) 224-5545; FAX (907) 224-5551
WEB SITE www.seward.net/glacierfresh
E-MAIL gfsfoods@artic.net

SIGNATURE PRODUCT **Natural smoked salmon**

NEWEST PRODUCT Canned Alaskan halibut
ADDITIONAL PRODUCTS Fresh and frozen halibut, salmon, rockfish, halibut cheeks, smoked salmon dips, and canned smoked salmon

Homarus, Inc.

76 Kisco Avenue
Mt. Kisco, NY 10549
PHONE (800) 23-SALMON; FAX (914) 666-8734

SIGNATURE PRODUCT **Smoked Norwegian salmon**

NEWEST PRODUCT Jumbo smoked trout
ADDITIONAL PRODUCTS Smoked pastrami salmon and other custom cures such as orange, lemon dill, and tequilla cilantro
COMMENTS *Definitely in the top four of the smoked salmons I've tried, very nice!*

※ **Horizon Foods**
Corporate Headquarters
Plainview, NY
PHONE (516) 937-1550
WEB SITE   www.horizonfoods.com

Horton's Naturally Smoked Seafoods

Gristmill Road, P.O. Box 430
Waterboro, ME 04087
PHONE (800) 346-6066; FAX (207) 247-6902
E-MAIL   Hortons@hortons.com

SIGNATURE PRODUCT   *Smoked Atlantic salmon*

ADDITIONAL PRODUCTS   Honey baked salmon, peppered salmon, pastrami salmon, bourbon-cured salmon, bluefish, catfish, trout, sturgeon, halibut, tuna, mackerel (all naturally smoked), as well as smoked mussels, scallops, and shrimp. Also various pates.

COMMENTS   *Of course the smoked salmon was very nice, but I really liked the tiny smoked shrimp and the salmon pate, both very special!*

Josephson's Smokehouse & Dock

106 Marine Drive, P.O. Box 412
Astoria, OR 97103
PHONE (800) 772-3474; FAX (503) 325-4075

SIGNATURE PRODUCT   *Scandinavian-style cold smoked salmon*

NEWEST PRODUCT   Hot smoked wine-maple chinook salmon and peppered, too

ADDITIONAL PRODUCTS   Hot smoked salmons, sturgeon, albacore tuna, black cod, halibut, trout, oyster, scallops, mussels, prawns, shark, cold smoked lox, salmon jerky, salmon pepper jerky, teriyaki salmon jerky, tuna strips, shark jerky, etc.

COMMENTS   *Usually I prefer the Atlantic salmons to the Pacific, particularly if it's cold smoked, but the Scandinavian-style cold smoked salmon from Josephson's was absolutely superb.*

Kasilof Fish Company

3912 - 134th Street NE
Marysville, WA 98271
PHONE (800) 322-7552; FAX (360) 653-3560
WEB SITE www.shopworks.com/kasilof/
E-MAIL kasilof@shopworks.com

SIGNATURE PRODUCT *Smoked Sockeye Salmon Fillet*

NEWEST PRODUCT   Garlic & Pepper Smoked King Salmon
ADDITIONAL PRODUCTS   Shelf-stable products: Smoked sockeye and
   Pacific salmon fillets in gift boxes smoked sockeye and Pacific salmon
   fillets in wooden gift boxes, smoked halibut, trout and mussels in gift
   boxes, smoked salmon pate, hard-smoked chinook, sockeye and more
COMMENTS   *Lovely smoked sockeye.*

Legal Seafoods — Fresh By Mail

33 Everett Street
Boston, MA 02134
PHONE (800) 343-5804; FAX (617) 254-5809
WEB SITE www.lsf.com

SIGNATURE PRODUCT *Maine Event Dinner for 2*

NEWEST PRODUCT   One-step Can Bake
ADDITIONAL PRODUCTS   LIVE lobsters, clambakes, chowders, fresh
   fish and shellfish
COMMENTS   *This is not just great lobster, clams or chowder; this is an
   EVENT. Legal Seafoods is a famous Boston seafood restaurant, they really
   know how to serve up great lobster. This is on the "must try" list, especially
   if you want an impressive, easy dinner.*

Nelson Crab Inc.

3088 Kindred Avenue, P.O. Box 520
Tokeland, WA 98590
PHONE (800) 262-0069; FAX (306) 267-2921

SIGNATURE PRODUCT *Dungeness crab*

NEWEST PRODUCT   Sockeye salmon
ADDITIONAL PRODUCTS   Tiny shrimp, smoked salmon, sturgeon, smoked crab legs, shad, shad roe, smoked shad roe pate, smoked albacore tuna, solid-style albacore tuna, chinook salmon, coho salmon, sockeye, salmon smoked oysters
COMMENTS   *Very nice canned fish products.*

Northern Discoveries Seafood
E. 5051 Grapeview Lp. Road, P.O. Box 310
Grapeview, WA 98546
PHONE (800) 843-6921; FAX (360) 275-7245
WEB SITE   smokedfish.com
E-MAIL   seafood@kendaco.telebyte.com

SIGNATURE PRODUCT   **Anniversary pack smoked salmon**

NEWEST PRODUCT   Honey-glazed salmon with secret spice glaze
ADDITIONAL PRODUCTS   Seafood gifts

Omaha Steaks
P.O. Box 3300
Omaha, NE 68103
PHONE (800) 228-9055; FAX (402) 597-8222
WEB SITE   www.omahasteaks.com
E-MAIL   info@omahasteaks.com

Oven Head Salmon Smokers

P.O. Box 455
St. George, New Brunswick CANADA EOG 2Y0
PHONE   (506) 755-2507;   FAX   (506) 755-8883

SIGNATURE PRODUCT   **Cold smoked salmon**

ADDITIONAL PRODUCTS   Salmon pate, salmon jerky
COMMENTS   *This is fabulous cold smoked Atlantic salmon. I recommend it highly and put it on my "must try" list.*

Santa's Smokehouse

2400 Davis Road
Fairbanks, AK 99701
PHONE (907) 456-3885; FAX (907) 456-3889
WEB SITE www.alaskasbest.com/fish

SIGNATURE PRODUCT **Salmon**

ADDITIONAL PRODUCTS Smoked salmon, salmon hot dogs, smoked
salmon sausage (two flavors), salmon burger patties, salmon hot links,
smoked halibut, smoked whitefish; also buffalo and reindeer meat
products and gift boxes available

Scottish Smoked Salmon Company

19112 Bloomfield Road
Olney, MD 20832
PHONE (800) 278-4050; FAX (301) 924-2085
WEB SITE http://www.salmonlady.com/feature.html
E-MAIL salmonlady@aol.com

SIGNATURE PRODUCT **Tobermory Scottish Smoked Salmon**

NEWEST PRODUCT Tobermory Smoked Salmon marinated in
Tobermory Single Malt Whisky
ADDITIONAL PRODUCTS Tobermory Smoked Trout (Red Rainbow);
Tobermory Gravelax Trout (Red Rainbow)
COMMENTS *This is lovely, delicate smoked salmon. I really liked the
Tobermory salmon marinated in the Tobermory single-malt scotch. This was
quite unusual and very special. On the "must try" list.*

Seabear

605 30th Street
Anacortes, WA 98221
PHONE (800) 645-FISH; FAX (360) 293-4097

SIGNATURE PRODUCT **Hot smoked salmon**

ADDITIONAL PRODUCTS Nova or Northwest style smoked salmon,
samplers, trios, smoked mussels and oysters

Seyco Fine Foods

970 E Santa Clara Street
Ventura, CA 93001-3033
PHONE (800) 423-2942; FAX (805) 641-9919
WEB SITE http://www.west.net/~adunstan/
E-MAIL adunstan@west.net

SIGNATURE PRODUCT **Premium Tuna**

NEWEST PRODUCT Ostrich Steaks
ADDITIONAL PRODUCTS The finest caviars of all types: King Crab, Lobster, Tuna. Candies, the finest meats of all types, hand-made pickles and relishes, tree-ripened fruits and hundreds more unique and hard-to-find fancy foods.

Shore to Door Seafood

5151 N.W. 17th Street
Margate, FL 33063
PHONE (800) 218-8147; FAX (954) 968-3201
WEB SITE www.shoretodoor.com; E-MAIL sales@shoretodoor.com

SIGNATURE PRODUCT **Fresh swordfish, tuna, mahimahi, salmon, etc.**

NEWEST PRODUCT Stone crab claws and soft-shell crab
ADDITIONAL PRODUCTS Smoked creole catfish, smoked peppered salmon, lobster, shrimp
COMMENTS *The fresh tuna steaks were very nice.*

Simply Shrimp

7794 N.W. 44th Street
Ft. Lauderdale, FL 33351
PHONE (800) 833-0888; FAX (954) 741-6127
WEB SITE www.ims-net.com/peddler/
E-MAIL peddlers@ix.netcom.com

SIGNATURE PRODUCT **Florida stone crab/farm-raised shrimp**

NEWEST PRODUCT Prepared fish and seafood
ADDITIONAL PRODUCTS Complete line of fresh fish, spreads, dips, soups, caviar, lobster tails, scallops, crab legs, etc.

Tsar Nicoulai Caviar

144 King Street
San Francisco, CA 94107
PHONE (800) 95-CAVIAR; FAX (415) 543-5172
WEB SITE www.Tsarnicoulai.com
E-MAIL caviar@crl.com

SIGNATURE PRODUCT **Giant Beluga Malossol**

NEWEST PRODUCT Giant Beluga Malossol
ADDITIONAL PRODUCTS Osefra caviar, sevruga caviar, American sturgeon caviar, salmon caviar, American golden caviar, and more

Vis Seafoods

2208 James Street, P.O. Box 31067
Bellingham, WA 98225
PHONE (888) 647-fish; FAX (360) 671-6847
WEB SITE www.visseafoods.com
E-MAIL fishhead@scruznet.com

SIGNATURE PRODUCT **Extra-fancy canned seafood**

NEWEST PRODUCT Garlic sockeye salmon, garlic pink salmon, cajun
pink salmon
ADDITIONAL PRODUCTS Smoked albacore, smoked oysters, dungeness crab, smoked and non-smoked salmon. Also through the mail;
fresh-frozen seafood: halibut, salmon, black cods, swordfish, rockfish,
crab. All fresh-frozen products are vacuum sealed.
CATALOG INFO The brochure tells us that "All salmon products are
harvested ourselves in Alaska."
COMMENTS *Vis has excellent products, very good quality, both the canned
and the smoked salmon (vacuum sealed) were great. The salmon was very
flavorful and good mixed with peas and pasta.*

Yukon River Salmon
733 West 4th Avenue #881
Anchorage, AK 99501
PHONE (907) 279-6519; FAX (907) 258-6688

SIGNATURE PRODUCT *Yukon River Keta salmon*

ADDITIONAL PRODUCTS Over 15 different salmon products produced: Keta salmon; fresh or frozen and in varying sizes. Also smoked
products and ikura and sjiko caviar.

SNACKS

Popcorn, nuts, and potato chips and other snackables.

 **1-800-GRANOLA**
P.O. Box 756
Amherst, MA 01004
PHONE (800) GRANOLA
WEB SITE www.800granola.com
E-MAIL info@800granola.com

A & B Milling Co.

200 Halifax Street, P.O. Box 327
Enfield, NC 27823
PHONE (800) 843-0101; FAX (919) 445-3163
WEB SITE auntrubyspeanuts.com
E-MAIL info@auntrubyspeanuts.com

SIGNATURE PRODUCT **Aunt Ruby's chocolate clusters**

NEWEST PRODUCT Aunt Ruby's roasted red skins
ADDITIONAL PRODUCTS Salted in shell, shelled raw peanuts,
    country-style cocktail peanuts, raw in shell, roasted in shell
COMMENTS *They're peanuts! I liked the roasted redskins.*

A Fine Nuthouse: Nuts4u

Nuts & Fruits & Gifts
P.O. Box 1864
Sugar Land, TX 77487
PHONE (800) 688-Nuts4u2 (688-7482); FAX (281) 242-2794
WEB SITE http://www.nuts4u.com; E-MAIL nuts4u@nuts4u.com

SIGNATURE PRODUCT **Gift tins: one, two and three pounds**

NEWEST PRODUCT Regal Mixed Nuts: cashews, almonds, pecans,
    macadamias & pistachio meats

ADDITIONAL PRODUCTS   Nuts, dried fruits, gift crystals. Gift tins: "Just" nut or fruit packs

All Hawaii Coffee
480 Kenolio Road #5-206
Kihei, HI 96753
PHONE (800) 565-2088; FAX (808) 875-4858
WEB SITE   www.mauigateway.com/~coffee/
E-MAIL   coffee@mauigateway.com

BKH Popcorn Inc.

504 West Highway 34
Phillips, NE 68865
PHONE (402) 886-2911; FAX (402) 886-2411
WEB SITE   http://www.4w.com/bkhpopcorn/
E-MAIL   bkhpopcorn@hamilton.net

SIGNATURE PRODUCT   **B.K. Heuermann's EXCLUSIVE microwave popcorn**

NEWEST PRODUCT   B.K. Heuermann's EXCLUSIVE microwave popcorn
ADDITIONAL PRODUCTS   We also sell bulk popping corn anywhere from one to 50 pounds.
COMMENTS   *This is really exceptional quality popcorn and if you are a connoisseur of the stuff, I'd definitely put it on the "must try" list.*

Ballreich's Potato Chips
186 Ohio Avenue, P.O. Box 186
Tiffin, OH 44883-0186
PHONE (800) 323-2447; FAX (419) 447-5635
WEB SITE   http://www.bpsom.com/ballreich/home.html
E-MAIL   ballreich@bpsom.com

SIGNATURE PRODUCT   **Regular "Marcelled" Potato Chips**

NEWEST PRODUCT   Southwestern BBQ Potato Chips
ADDITIONAL PRODUCTS   Bar-B-Q Potato Chips, Sour Cream & Onion Potato Chips, Salt & Vinegar Potato Chips, No-Salt Added Potato Chips

COMMENTS   *Liked all the flavors but am a bit of a traditionalist and liked the regular "marcelled" chip the best.*

Bates Nut Farm
15954 Woodsvalley Road
Valley Center, CA 92082
PHONE (760) 749-3333; FAX (760) 749-9499

SIGNATURE PRODUCT   **Nuts, dried fruits, candy**

ADDITIONAL PRODUCTS   Jams, jellies, teas, sauces, dates, granola

Big Lou Enterprises
5805 N. Cherub Lane, P.O. Box 247
Atwater, CA 95301; Winton, CA 95388
PHONE (209) 573-8121; FAX (209) 358-3600
WEB SITE   http://www.biglou.com
E-MAIL   biglou@fia.net

SIGNATURE PRODUCT   **Gift Box of Flavored Pistachios (6-8 oz. bags)**

NEWEST PRODUCT   Gift Box of Flavored Pistachios (6-8 oz. bags)
ADDITIONAL PRODUCTS   Garlic, jalapeno, nacho cheese, cinnamon toffee, chili lemon, and cajun barbecue flavored pistachios
COMMENTS   *The garlic and chili lemon were my favorites as well as, of course, plain ol' pistachios.*

The Blazing Chile Brothers
985 Quarry Street
Petaluma, CA 94954
PHONE (800) 473-9040; FAX (415) 332-1238
WEB SITE   www.chilebros.com; E-MAIL Blazing@chilebros.com

China Ranch Date Farm
#8 China Ranch Road
Tecopa, CA 92389
PHONE (760) 852-4415

▦ *Coyote Moon*

1709 South Braddick Avenue
Pittsburgh, PA 15218
PHONE (412) 594-4830; FA   (412) 242-8710
WEB SITE   spicyhot.com/coyotemoon/
E-MAIL   coyote@spicyhot.com

▦ *Dave's Gourmet Inc.*

1255 Montgomery Avenue
San Bruno, CA 94066
PHONE (800) 758-0372; FAX (415) 794-0340
WEB SITE   davesgourmet.com; E-MAIL insanity@davesgourmet.com

▦ *Easy Exchange — "Snack 15"*

P.O. Box 525
Crugars, NY 10521
PHONE (800) 832-8990; FAX   (914) 739-7541

▦ *Farm2You*

P.O. Box 9146
Chico, CA 95927
PHONE (888) FARM2YOU; FAX (916) 865-4929
WEB SITE   http://www.farm2you.com
E-MAIL   steve@farm2you.com

Great American Popcorn Company

311 S. Main Street
Galena, IL 61036
PHONE (800) 814-9494; FAX (815) 777-4118
WEB SITE   www.popcorn.com
E-MAIL   popcorn1.galenalink.com

SIGNATURE PRODUCT   *100 flavors of popcorn*

NEWEST PRODUCT   Coronary Cookies and Mississippi Mud Puppies
ADDITIONAL PRODUCTS   In addition to flavored popcorns and
  gourmet cookies, unique chocolate items, monster pretzels, killer
  pretzels, giant tiggers and more

COMMENTS *It's popcorn . . . and in every flavor you can imagine and more! (Still like the caramel corn the best, guess I'm not very imaginative.)*

Harry and David
2518 S. Pacific Highway, P.O. Box 712
Medford, OR 97501
PHONE (800) 547-3033; FAX (800) 648-6640
WEB SITE www.harryanddavid.com

Heaton Pecan Farm
309 Sunrise Boulevard
Clanton, AL 35045
PHONE (800) 446-3531; FAX (205) 755-8677

SIGNATURE PRODUCT **Pecans**

ADDITIONAL PRODUCTS Candies with pecans, toppings, jams, syrups, pecan honey butter and gift baskets

COMMENTS *Lovely pecans!*

Hors d' Oeuvres Unlimited
4209 Dell Avenue, P.O. Box 31
North Bergen, NJ 07047
PHONE (800) 648-3787; FAX (201) 865-1175

SIGNATURE PRODUCT *Hors d'oeuvres*

ADDITIONAL PRODUCTS Literally hundreds of cold and hot hors d'oeuvres from pigs in a blanket to brie and apricot encroute

House Of Fire
1108 Spruce Street
Boulder, CO 80302
PHONE (800) 717-5787; FAX (303) 447-8685
WEB SITE www.houseoffire.com
E-MAIL info@houseoffire.com

How Sweet It Is!

P.O. Box 376
Jenkintown, PA 19046
PHONE (215) 784-9980; FAX (215) 784-0761
WEB SITE www.howsweet.com
E-MAIL tomgold@vikingcomputers.com

Humpty Dumpty Potato Chip Company

P.O. Box 2247
South Portland, ME 04116-2247
PHONE (800) 274-2447; FAX (207) 885-0773
WEB SITE www.humptydumpty.com

SIGNATURE PRODUCT *Bar-B-Que Chips. The HD Chip Collection*

NEWEST PRODUCT Pretzels, fries, Low-fat tortilla, etc.
ADDITIONAL PRODUCTS Our collector tins filled with a variety of different flavors; case of 6 oz. product in various flavors; our QVC package; our tin filled with 30 1-oz. bags; our vend-pack; box of 36 1-oz. bags; ties; hats

International Nut Company

5 South, Box 540
Walpole, MA 02081
PHONE (800) 710-9380; FAX (508) 660-8972
WEB SITE www.inter-nut.com
E-MAIL nuts@inter-nut.com

SIGNATURE PRODUCT *Best Imported Pistachios*

NEWEST PRODUCT Jumbo Roasted & Salted Turkish Pistachios
ADDITIONAL PRODUCTS Gourmet trail mix, huge cashews, custom imprinted wood gift crates packed with your choice of our fabulous nuts. Promotional corporate gifts
COMMENTS *These are absolutely perfect pistachios in my mind and on my "must try" list.*

Krema Nut Company

1000 W. Goodale Boulevard
Columbus, OH 43212
PHONE (614) 299-4131; FAX (614) 299-1636
WEB SITE www.krema.com; E-MAIL nuts@krema.com

SIGNATURE PRODUCT **Cashew butter, almond butter**

NEWEST PRODUCT Cashew crunch candy
ADDITIONAL PRODUCTS Peanut butter, hot & spicy; peanut butter
caramel corn; hot & spicy caramel corn; all roasted nut meats; giant
Krema cashews
COMMENTS *Both the almond butter and the cashew butter were great on
crackers as an hors' doeuvre or snack. Very tasty!*

Lou-retta's Custom Chocolates Inc.

3764 Harlem Road
Buffalo, NY 14215
PHONE (716) 833-7111; FAX (716) 833-4260
WEB SITE www.louretta.com; E-MAIL Loretta K@aol.com

SIGNATURE PRODUCT **Chocolate Laced Popcorn**

NEWEST PRODUCT Buffalo Gold (pretzel nuggets w/ golddust)
COMMENTS *I liked the pretzels.*

Madly Pop'n

148 N. Oak Park Avenue
Oak Park, IL 60301
PHONE (800) 774-5620; FAX (708) 386-7904
WEB SITE www.madlypopn.com; E-MAIL rachel@madlypopn.com

SIGNATURE PRODUCT **Handpainted gift tins of popcorn**

NEWEST PRODUCT Decorative gift boxes filled with popcorn and
chocolates
ADDITIONAL PRODUCTS Twenty-four flavors of popcorn and
chocolate-covered pretzels, chocolate amaretto pecans, butter toffee
peanuts, assorted chocolates and nuts

COMMENTS   *Liked the Cheezy Cheddar popcorn (I'm a traditionalist when it comes to popcorn).*

Marmix Company

P.O. Box 1458
Newport Beach, CA 92659-0458
PHONE (888) 627-4649; FAX (714) 673-1927
WEB SITE   www.marimix.com

SIGNATURE PRODUCT   **Gourmet Cereal Snack Mixes**

ADDITIONAL PRODUCTS   Honey Vanola, Mystic Maple, Original Peanut Butter N' Cinnamon; all cereal/granola mixes with various flavorings and nuts
COMMENTS   *These are exceptional "snacks" that definitely take the junk out of junk food. They are delightful and tasty, particularly liked Honey Vanola.*

Mary of Puddin Hill

4007 Interstate 30, P.O. Box 241
Greensville, TX 75403-0241
PHONE (800) 545-8889; FAX (903) 455-4522

Mauna Loa Macadamia Nuts

6523 North Galena Road, P.O. Box 1772
Peoria, IL 61656
PHONE (800) 832-9993; FAX (309) 689-3893
WEB SITE   www.maunaloa.com

SIGNATURE PRODUCT   **Macadamia nuts**

NEWEST PRODUCT   Chocolate covered macadamia nuts
ADDITIONAL PRODUCTS   Gift baskets, nuts, chocolates, and Kona coffee

Naturally Nuts & Fruity Too!

21661 Avenue 296
Execter, CA 93221
PHONE (209) 477-9569
WEB SITE   http://members.aol.com/nnuts/nnuts.htm

E-MAIL   nnuts@aol.com

SIGNATURE PRODUCT   *Dried Kiwi, Persimmon and Tomato*

ADDITIONAL PRODUCTS   Dried Apples, dried cranberries, almonds, pinenuts, pistachios, walnut meat. We have available to us a large variety of other dried fruits and nuts.

COMMENTS   *Really nice dried fruit; was surprised how much I liked the dried kiwi.*

Nick's Nuts, "Your Full Service Nut House"

2691-B Peachtree Square
Atlanta, GA 30360
PHONE (888) 642-5768; FAX (770) 455-4303
WEB SITE http://www.nicksnuts.com; E-MAIL nick@nicksnuts.com

SIGNATURE PRODUCT   *Premium Jr. Mammoth Pecan Halves smothered in rich natural chocolate*

NEWEST PRODUCT   Jumbo Cashews smothered in rich natural chocolate

ADDITIONAL PRODUCTS   Seventh Heaven (7 flavorful pecan varieties); premium pecan sampler (larger portion of 6 varietes in 7th Heaven); Executive Gift Tray (3 lbs./4 oz. offering of 3 flavored pecans, jumbo cashews and large pecan log roll); home-style peanuts and more

COMMENTS   *The chocolate cashews are good.*

Off The Deep End

712 East Street
Frederick, MD 21701
PHONE (800) 248-045; FAX (301) 698-0375
WEB SITE   http://www.offthedeepend.com
E-MAIL   chilimon@offthedeepend.com

The Olive Connection

21661 Avenue 296
Exeter, CA 93221
PHONE (209) 477-9569
WEB SITE   http://members.aol.com/olivcon/olive.htm
E-MAIL   olivecon@aol.com

▩ ORE-ASIA

4651 NE Riverside Drive
McMinnville, OR 97128
PHONE (503) 434-9766; FAX (503) 434-2809
WEB SITE www.ore-asia.com
E-MAIL info@ore-asia.com

The Peanut Patch Inc.

🍴

27478 Southampton Parkway, P.O. Box 186
Courtland, VA 23837
PHONE (800) 544-0896; FAX (757) 653-9530
WEB SITE www.peanutpatch.com; E-MAIL peanutpatch@gc.net

SIGNATURE PRODUCT **Gourmet Home Cooked Peanuts**

NEWEST PRODUCT Cajun Spiced Peanuts
ADDITIONAL PRODUCTS Super extra large homecooked Virginia type
  peanuts in salted, unsalted, redskins and cajun spiced. Peanut brittle,
  butter toffee peanuts, chocolate-covered peanuts (October to May),
  old-fashioned peanuts, squares, cashew brittle, raw peanuts and more
COMMENTS *I really like those big Virginia peanuts!*

▩ Philly Food Division of Dial-A-Party Catering

107 S. Monroe Street
Media, PA 19063
PHONE (610) 565-4386; FAX (610) 566-8200
WEB SITE http://www.phillypretzels.com
E-MAIL philly@inet.net

▩ Piquant Pepper

P.O. Box 20196
Wichita, KS 67208-1196
PHONE (800) 931-7474; FAX (316) 685-9144
WEB SITE www.shipnizzy.com
E-MAIL piquant@dtc.net

The Popcorn Factory
13970 W. Laurel Drive
Lake Forest, IL 60045
PHONE (800) 541-2676; FAX (309) 689-3885
WEB SITE   www.popcornfactory.com

SIGNATURE PRODUCT   *Exclusive decoratives with fresh popcorn*

NEWEST PRODUCT   Selections from our O!ccasions catalog
ADDITIONAL PRODUCTS   Gift baskets, gifts for all occasions: Birthday,
thank-you, new baby, congratulations, get well, etc.

PopcornJunction
4626 Coldwater Road
Fort Wayne, IN 46825
PHONE (219) 484-4696
WEB SITE   home1.gte.net/fortcorn; E-MAIL fortcorn@gte.net

SIGNATURE PRODUCT   Vanilla Butternut

NEWEST PRODUCT   Apple Julyacks
ADDITIONAL PRODUCTS   Vanilla butternut, praline with pecans, butter rum, butterscotch, Dutch apple, green apple, cocky pop, caramel w/
cashews or peanuts, Cajun, sour cream & chives, taco, white cheddar and
many more flavors

POP 'N STUFF INC.
Broadway at the Beach, 1303 Celebrity Circle 125
Myrtle Beach, SC 29577
PHONE (800) 735-5440; FAX (803) 946-6813
WEB SITE   http://sccoast.net/popn/popnstuf/home.htm:
E-MAIL   popn@sccoast.net

SIGNATURE PRODUCT   *Flavored popcorn, candies, other foods*

NEWEST PRODUCT   Keylime Flavored Popcorn
ADDITIONAL PRODUCTS   Flavored popcorn, candy, jellies & jams as
well as coffee, sauces and other items . . . a flavor emporium. All of
our products and gifts can be shipped world-wide from our store in
Myrtle Beach, South Carolina.

COMMENTS *The bagged popcorn was even packed for shipping loose in (old) popcorn! Great stuff!*

Priesters Pecan Co.

227 Old Fort Drive, P.O. Box 381
Fort Deposit, AL 36032
PHONE (800) 277-3226; FAX (334) 227-4294
WEB SITE www.priester.com

SIGNATURE PRODUCT *Old-fashioned pecan pie*

NEWEST PRODUCT Blackberry wine cake
ADDITIONAL PRODUCTS Roasted salted pecans, natural pecans,
Divinity fudge, pecan logs, Bravo brownies
COMMENTS *The sample-ette of pecan pie was fine, the blackberry wine cake is for someone with a major sweet tooth.*

Rural Route 1 Popcorn

11623 Highway 80 N
Livingston, WI 53554
PHONE (800) 828-8115; FAX (608) 943-6438
WEB SITE www.ruralroute1.com; E-MAIL pops@ruralroute1.com

SIGNATURE PRODUCT *Ivory Almond K'nuckle*

NEWEST PRODUCT Cashew chocolate — caramel corn and cashews
covered with fudge
ADDITIONAL PRODUCTS Combination decorative tins, create your own
by choosing flavors: cheese corn, vanilla black walnut, deluxe caramel
corn with pecans and more. Also, microwave popcorn in butter, butter
light, and natural flavors — white, yellow, red, black. Toppings and gifts.
COMMENTS *The K'nuckle is wild . . . truly nuts, popcorn and candy in one!*

San Angel

668 Worcester Road
Stowe, VT 05672
PHONE (800) 598-6448
E-MAIL dpeet@pwshift

Stahmann's

P.O. Box 130
San Miguel, NM 88058-0130
PHONE (800) 654-6887; FAX (505) 526-7824
WEB SITE www.stahmanns.com

SIGNATURE PRODUCT *Farm fresh pecans*

NEWEST PRODUCT Pecan crunch
ADDITIONAL PRODUCTS Gourmet nut confections such as pecan brittle, chile pecan brittle, milk chocolate pecan bark, pecan clusters, pistachio crunch with white chocolate. Plus, fresh baked pies, caramel pecan corn and more
COMMENTS *The pecan crunch is mighty tasty.*

Sweet Energy

4 Acorn Lane
Colchester, VT 05446
PHONE (800) 979-3380; FAX (802) 655-1372

Totally Nuts Company

7 Wirt Street
New Brunswick, NJ 08901
PHONE (800) 639-NUTS; FAX (908) 249-5228
WEB SITE www.totallynuts.com
E-MAIL jester@totallynuts.com

SIGNATURE PRODUCT *Certified Nut Case (gourmet assortment of nuts)*

NEWEST PRODUCT "High Fiver" Certified Nutcase (5 most popular nuts)
ADDITIONAL PRODUCTS Other certified Nutcases: Shell Shocker (4 varieties flavored in-shell peanuts); Major Mix-up (11 varieties of nuts) Peanut Gallery (11 varieties of peanuts), Sack-In-The-Box (3 lbs. of flavored in-shell peanuts or 4.5 lbs. pistachios in burlap sack)
COMMENTS *As someone who favors plain nuts over flavored, I was surprisingly impressed with both their honey cashews and their amaretto pecan. Very high quality. They're the nuts!*

Triple A Pistachios

Rt. 1, Box 52
Cochise, AZ 85606
PHONE (800) 442-4207; FAX (520) 826-3128
WEB SITE www.Tuscon.com/pistachios

SIGNATURE PRODUCT **Pistachios**

ADDITIONAL PRODUCTS Pistachios in a variety of flavors and containers: lemon/lime, garlic, Southwest (spicy) and plain
COMMENTS *Very nice big pistachios and I liked the garlic flavored even though the plain will always be my favorite.*

Twin Peaks Gourmet Trading Post

725 Burnett Avenue #6
San Francisco, CA 94131
PHONE (888) 4TPEAKS (487-3257); FAX (415) 824-7849
WEB SITE http://tpeaks.com
E-MAIL gourmet@tpeaks.com

Virginia Diner

P.O. Box 1030
Wakefield, VA 23888
PHONE (800) 868-6887; FAX (757) 899-2281
WEB SITE www.vadiner.com
E-MAIL vadiner@infi.net

SIGNATURE PRODUCT **Gourmet peanuts**

NEWEST PRODUCT 1 1/2 lbs. Old Bay Peanuts
ADDITIONAL PRODUCTS Complete line of peanuts; plus peanut brittle, pecans, desserts, peanut butter, salsa, sauces, hams, preserves and gift baskets
COMMENTS *Before I sampled the peanuts from Virginia Diner I thought the concept of gourmet peanuts was an oxymoron. These are truly exceptional peanuts and are on the "must try" list.*

▦ *Yasmin Gourmet Food*
56 Pleasant Street
Greenville, RI 02828-1920
PHONE (401) 949-2121; FAX (401) 949-0991
WEB SITE   hudson.idt.net/~brbina19/
E-MAIL   bobbybina@hotmail.com

VEGETABLES

Every variety of fresh vegetable from asparagus to onions and also pickled items, mushrooms, truffles, and olives.

3E Market
6753 Jones Mill Court, Suite A
Norcross, GA 30136
PHONE (800) 333-5548; FAX (800) 343-2652
WEB SITE http://www.3emarket.com; E-MAIL market@3e.com

AlpineAire Foods
P.O. Box 926
Nevada City, CA 95959
PHONE (800) FAB-MEAL; FAX (916) 272-2624

Bland Farms

P.O. Box 506-PG19
Glenndale, GA 30427
PHONE (800) 843-2542; FAX (912) 654-1330
WEB SITE www.blandfarms.com

SIGNATURE PRODUCT **Vidalia sweet onions**

NEWEST PRODUCT Vidalia sweet onion & peach salsa
ADDITIONAL PRODUCTS Vidalia sweet onion dressings, relishes, preserves, and jellies, Southern cakes and pies, cookies and candies
COMMENTS *The Southern lemon cheese cake (really a many-layered cake) was divine. Very good viniagrettes, too. And loved the Vidalia onion relish, of course!*

Callaway Gardens
P.O. Box 2000
Pine Mountain, GA 31822-2000
PHONE (800) 280-7524; FAX (706) 663-5058

Coyote Moon

1709 South Braddick Avenue
Pittsburgh, PA 15218
PHONE (412) 594-4830; FA (412) 242-8710
WEB SITE spicyhot.com/coyotemoon/
E-MAIL coyote@spicyhot.com

Cushman's

3325 Forest Hill Boulevard
West Palm Beach, FL 33406
PHONE (800) 776-7575; FAX (800) 776-4329
E-MAIL cushman@aol.com

Delftree Mushrooms

234 Union Street
North Adams, MA 02147
PHONE (800) 243-3742; FAX (413) 664-4908

SIGNATURE PRODUCT **Fresh shiitake mushrooms**

NEWEST PRODUCT Shiitake mushroom marinade
ADDITIONAL PRODUCTS A full line of dried wild mushrooms, books, soups, and sauces

Diamond Organics

P.O. Box 2159
Freedom, CA 95019
PHONE (888) ORGANIC; FAX (888) 888-6777
WEB SITE www.diamondorganics.com
E-MAIL Organics@diamondorganics.com

SIGNATURE PRODUCT **The Original Organic Fruit & Veggie Sampler**

NEWEST PRODUCT Diamondbars — totally organic energy bar
ADDITIONAL PRODUCTS A complete year-round selection of the freshest, best tasting, organically grown fruits, vegetables, flowers & more. Delivered direct to home cooks nationwide. No minimum order, order exactly what you need

COMMENTS   *This produce is extraordinary and is definitely on the "must try" list. Even if you don't want to eat it, just to look at it gives you a lift and a breath of fresh air . . . but do be sure to eat it, too. It's fantastic!*

Diane's Gourmet Luxuries
11121 N. Rodney Parhan
Little Rock, AR 72212
PHONE (501) 224-2639; FAX (501) 224-8921
WEB SITE www.dianes-gourmet.com
E-MAIL   diane@diane-gourmet.com

Earthy Delights Inc.
4180 Keller Road, Suite B
Holt, MI 48842
PHONE (800) 367-4709; FAX (517) 699-1750
WEB SITE   http://www.earthy.com
E-MAIL   ed@earthy.com

SIGNATURE PRODUCT   **Fresh Wild Mushrooms**

NEWEST PRODUCT   Pumpkin Seed Oil
ADDITIONAL PRODUCTS   Morels, fiddleheads, wild leeks, chanterelles, cepes (Porcini), matsutake, clamshell, mushroom, baby blue oyster, trumpet, royale pom pom, blanc cinnamon cap, premium shiitake, woodear, enoki, black trumpets, dried tart cherries, and more

Farmers Pick Specialty Garlic
10400 Overland Road #393
Boise, ID 83709
PHONE (208) 333-0066
WEB SITE   http://www.farmerspick.com
E-MAIL   paul@farmerspick.com

SIGNATURE PRODUCT   **Fresh garlic**

ADDITIONAL PRODUCTS   Farmers Pick offers a full line of fresh specialty garlic including elephant garlic, organically-grown harneck varieties, super colossal size heads of garlic and braids and wreaths. Chili pepper Ristras, too!

Florida Fruit Shippers

5006 Gulfport Boulevard S
Gulfport, FL 33707
PHONE (800) 715-8279; FAX (813) 323-5412
WEB SITE www.orangesonline.com; E-MAIL ffs@orangesonline

Flying Noodle

1 Arrowhead Road
Duxbury, MA 02332
PHONE (800) 566-0599; FAX (617) 934-1527
WEB SITE www.flyingnoodle.com
E-MAIL bigparmesan@flyingnoodle.com

Frieda's Inc.

4465 Corporate Center Drive
Los Alamitos, CA 90720
PHONE (800) 241-1771; FAX (714) 816-0273
WEB SITE www.friedas.com
E-MAIL mail@friedas.com

The Gourmet Trading Company

1071 Avenida Acaso
Camarillo, CA 93012
PHONE (800) 888-3484; FAX (805) 389-4790
WEB SITE www.gourmettrader.com
E-MAIL trader@gourmettrader.com

Harry and David

2518 S. Pacific Highway, P.O. Box 712
Medford, OR 97501
PHONE (800) 547-3033; FAX (800) 648-6640
WEB SITE www.harryanddavid.com

Hosgood's Company

P.O. Box 1265
Strafford, TX 77497-1265
PHONE (800) 4-GARLIC
WEB SITE www.4garlic.com

▓ *Jane Butel's Pecos Valley Spice*
2429 Monroe Street, N.E.
Albuquerque, NM 87110
PHONE (800) 473-TACO; FAX (505) 888-4269

▓ *Los Chileros de Nuevo Mexico*
P.O. Box 6215
Sante Fe, NM 87502
PHONE (505) 471-6967; FAX (505) 473-7306
WEB SITE www.hotchilepepper.com/ordering.htm

▓ *Mid-Atlantic Food*
280 West Avenue
Long Beach, NJ 07740
PHONE (800) 748-3644; FAX (908) 229-2964
WEB SITE www.virtualfoods.com
E-MAIL pdelgand@mars.superlink.net

Miss Scarlet
1339 Rollins Road, P.O. Box 1488
Burlingame, CA 94010
PHONE (800) 345-6734; FAX (415) 340-9680

SIGNATURE PRODUCT **Marinated vegetables**

ADDITIONAL PRODUCTS Very extensive line of marinated vegetables
from stuffed marinated eggplant, dilled snow peas and Brussel sprouts
to pitted clamata olive . . . and much more

Mister Spear

1004 Navy Drive, P.O. Box 1768
Stockton, CA 95201
PHONE (800) 677-7327; FAX (209) 464-3846

SIGNATURE PRODUCT **Fresh asparagus**

NEWEST PRODUCT Organic salad sampler

ADDITIONAL PRODUCTS   Artichokes, avacados, shiitake mushrooms, stringless sugar snap peas, bing cherries, super sweet corn, red ripe tomatoes, summer beans, mini veggies, fugi apples

COMMENTS   *Very extraordinary vegetables, like nothing we can buy in a super market. The asparagus are really something special and are a Spring "must buy."*

The Oriental Pantry
423 Great Road
Acton, MA 01720
PHONE (800) 828-0368; FAX (617) 275-4506
WEB SITE   www.orientalpantry.com
E-MAIL   oriental@orientalpantry.com

Panola Pepper Corp.
Route 2, Box 148
Lake Providence, LA 71254
PHONE (800) 256-3013; FAX (318) 559-3003
WEB SITE   www.southernnet.com/panola_peppers

Pezzini Farms
460 Nashua Road, P.O. Box 1276
Castroville, CA 95012
PHONE (800) 347-6118; FAX (408) 757-4476
WEB SITE   www.pezzinifarms.com
E-MAIL   artichoke@pezzinifarms.com

SIGNATURE PRODUCT   **Fresh artichokes**

NEWEST PRODUCT   Artichoke spread

ADDITIONAL PRODUCTS   Vegetable dips: lemon dill, garlic-dijon, sweet red pepper, honey-sesame, onion-herb, pestos: artichoke pesto sauce, artichoke marinara, artichoke primavera, gourmet pastas, pasta sauce, fresh produce and a variety of gourmet foods and gift baskets

The Olive Connection

21661 Avenue 296
Exeter, CA 93221
PHONE (209) 477-9569
WEB SITE http://members.aol.com/olivcon/olive.htm
E-MAIL olivecon@aol.com

SIGNATURE PRODUCT *Garlic Stuffed Olive*

ADDITIONAL PRODUCTS We carry 39 whole, pitted or stuffed green
olives

The Pikled Garlik

P.O. Box 846
Pacific Grove, CA 93950
PHONE (800) 775-9788; FAX (408) 393-1709

SIGNATURE PRODUCT *Pikled garlik*

NEWEST PRODUCT Fruity salsa
ADDITIONAL PRODUCTS Gift packs, cookbook, garlic-related kitchen
gadgets
COMMENTS *Love garlic and their Saucy Salsa.*

▦ R.L. Pearson & Sons

P.O. Box 1892
Winter Haven, FL 33883-1892
PHONE (888) 438-3565
WEB SITE www.juiceking.com
E-MAIL info@juiceking.com

Santa Barbara Olive Co.

3280 Calzada, P.O. Box 1570
Santa Ynez, CA 93460
PHONE (800) 624-4896; FAX (805) 686-1659

SIGNATURE PRODUCT *Jalapeno stuffed olives*

NEWEST PRODUCT Sun-dried tomato stuffed olives

ADDITIONAL PRODUCTS   Salsas, pasta and pesto sauces, herbed oil, spiced and stuffed olives

COMMENTS   *The garlic stuffed olives are fabulous and make a gin martini even better tasting, if that's possible!*

▒ Sultan's Delight
P.O. Box 090302
Brooklyn, NY 11209
PHONE (800) 852-5046; FAX (718) 745-2563

▒ Superbly Southwestern
2400 Rio Grande NW #1-171
Albuquerque, NM 87104
PHONE (800) 467-4HOT
WEB SITE   www.hotchile.com; E-MAIL   hotchile@aol.com

Timber Crest Farms
4791 Dry Creek Road
Healdsburg, CA 95448
PHONE (707) 433-8251; FAX (707) 433-8255
WEB SITE   www.timbercrest.com/tcf/
E-MAIL   tcf@timbercrest.com

SIGNATURE PRODUCT   **Dried tomatoes**

NEWEST PRODUCT   Muffaletta

ADDITIONAL PRODUCTS   Marinated tomatoes with roasted garlic, dried tomato pesto, dried tomato tapenade, tossta and whole dried fruit line

COMMENTS   *The dried tomato tapenade is wonderful on a little French bread with a bit of goat cheese.*

Veggie Express
P.O. Box 29
Sycamore, GA 31790
PHONE (888) 834-4439 or 888-veggiex; FAX (912) 387-6606
WEB SITE   www.veggieexpress.com
E-MAIL   info@veggieexpress.com

SIGNATURE PRODUCT   *Fresh produce*

ADDITIONAL PRODUCTS   Apples, broccoli, green bell pepper, red bell pepper, cauliflower, cucumber, eggplant, greenbeans, red & white grapefruit, onions, oranges, pole beans, long hot pepper, finger hot pepper, jalapeno pepper, butternut squash, straight-neck squash

Yasmin Gourmet Food
56 Pleasant Street
Greenville, RI 02828-1920
PHONE (401) 949-2121; FAX (401) 949-0991
WEB SITE   hudson.idt.net/~brbina19/
E-MAIL   bobbybina@hotmail.com

ETHNIC & REGIONAL FOODS

AMISH

Birky's Cafe
205 South Main, Kouts, IN 46347
PHONE (219) 766-3851
WEB SITE birkycafe.com
E-MAIL jay@birkycafe.com

SIGNATURE PRODUCT **Amish Style Apple Butter**

NEWEST PRODUCT Birky's Barbeque Sauce
ADDITIONAL PRODUCTS Amish noodles, cookbooks, Indiana Honey

 ### Gifts from the Illinois Amish Country
138 S. Vine
Arthur, IL 61911
PHONE (800) 879-2494; FAX (217) 543-2898
WEB SITE www.IllinoisAmishCountry.com/WLPantry/gifthome.htm
E-MAIL AmishCM@net66.com

AUSTRALIAN

 ### Big Betty's
P.O. Box 531
Glenorchy, Tasmania AUSTRALIA 7010
PHONE (61) 36261-3296;   FAX   (61) 36261-3296
WEB SITE www.ozemail.com.au/~bbetty's
E-MAIL bbettys@ozemail.com.au

▦ Rainforest Honey Co.
314 Colby Drive
Dartmouth, Nova Scotia CANADA B2V 2B6
PHONE (902) 462-0680; FAX (902) 462-0680
WEB SITE   http://www.isisnet.com/MAX/ads/honey.html
E-MAIL   rainforesthoneyco@ns.sympatico.ca

▦ Wescobee Limited
6053 Western Australia, P.O. Box 105
Perth, WA WESTERN AUSTRALIA
PHONE 08 92718133; FAX 08 92711025
WEB SITE   http://kite.ois.net.au/~eduard/
E-MAIL   eduard@ois.net.au

BRITISH

The British Gourmet
45 Wall Street
Madison, CT 06443
PHONE (800) 842-6674; FAX (203) 245-3477
WEB SITE   www.thebritishshoppe.com
E-MAIL   gourmet@thebritisheshoppe.com

SIGNATURE PRODUCT   *Tea*

NEWEST PRODUCT   Wensleydale cheese
ADDITIONAL PRODUCTS   One of the largest selections of gourmet and
traditional British food, cheeses, teas, and gifts available

▦ Dunns Seafare
Jamestown Business Park, Finglas
Dublin, IRELAND 11
PHONE 00-353-1-8643100; FAX 00-353-1-8643109
WEB SITE   www/clubi.ie/dunns-seafare
E-MAIL   dunns@clubi.ie

Queen Square Delicatessen
20 Queen Square
Cambridge, Ontario   CANADA N1S-1H3
PHONE (888) 230-2656; FAX (519) 622-2613
WEB SITE   www.queensquare.com
E-MAIL   info@queensquare.com

CAJUN

Alex Patout's Louisiana Foods
221 Royal Street
New Orleans, LA 70130
PHONE (504)525-7788; FAX (504)525-7809
WEB SITE   patout.com
E-MAIL   patout.com

SIGNATURE PRODUCT   *Quality Frozen Louisiana Food*

NEWEST PRODUCT   Smoked Pork Roast
ADDITIONAL PRODUCTS   Chicken & Andouille Gumbo with Rice;
    Seafood Gumbo with Rice; Red Beans with Andouille; Sausage
    Crawfish Etouffee; Creole Mustard Viniagrette; Cajun Seasoning

Cajun Cooking Supplies
515 Bordeaux Street
New Orleans, LA 70115
PHONE (504) 891-1660; FAX: (504) 897-2760
WEB SITE   http://www.mindspring.com/~glr/cajun/
E-MAIL   glr@mindspring.com

SIGNATURE PRODUCT   *Cajun supplies*

▓ *Fruge Aquafarms*
525 E. 8th Street
Crowley, LA 70526
PHONE (888) 254-8626
WEB SITE www.cajuncrawfish.com
E-MAIL cajuncrawfish@worldnet.att.com

Gazin's

2910 Toulouse Street, P.O. Box 19221
New Orleans, LA 70119-0221
PHONE (800) 262-6410; FAX (504) 827-5319

SIGNATURE PRODUCT **Cajun/Creole foods**

ADDITIONAL PRODUCTS Many lovely Cajun items from fresh bread to
Creole sauce.
CATALOG INFO Very nice catalog that also has copper cookware
COMMENTS *I liked the cajun sauce but the fig preserves were exceptional.*

Magic Seasonings
New Orleans, LA 70123
PHONE (800) 457-2857; FAX (501) 731-3579
WEB SITE www.chefpaul.com; E-MAIL info@chefpaul.com

SIGNATURE PRODUCT **Chef Paul Prudhomme's Magic Seasoning
Blends**

NEWEST PRODUCT Magic Seasoning Salt
ADDITIONAL PRODUCTS Chef Paul's cookbooks, andouille and tasso
(seasoned and smoked meats), sweet potato pecan pie (from K-Paul's
restaurant), cast-iron cookware, seasoning blend gift packs
COMMENTS *He's famous for Cajun and with good reason.*

Louisiana French Market Online
4614 Tupello Street
Baton Rouge, LA 70808
PHONE (504) 928-1428; FAX (504) 774-4085
WEB SITE http://www.louisianafrenchmarket.com
E-MAIL service@louisianafrenchmarket.com

SIGNATURE PRODUCT *Louisiana/Cajun coffees, seasonings and food mixes*

NEWEST PRODUCT Hot sauces

ADDITIONAL PRODUCTS We also carry cookbooks, pre-seasoned iron pots and King Cakes

▦ **Rao's Bakery**
2596 Calder
Beaumont, TX 77702
PHONE (800) 831-3098; FAX (409) 832-2011
WEB SITE www.setexas.com/raos
E-MAIL Raosbakery@aol.com

CENTRAL AMERICAN

▦ **Blue Zebu Fine Coffee**
2820 Camino Del Rio South, Suite 204 A
San Diego, CA 92108
PHONE (619) 645-8955; FAX (619) 296-6578
WEB SITE www.bluezebu.com
E-MAIL bluezebu@cts.com

▦ **Cafe Rico**
Caparra Heights Station, P.O. Box 11959
San Juan, PR 00922
PHONE (787) 782-0620; FAX (787) 793-8177
WEB SITE www.caferico.com
E-MAIL info@caferico.com

▦ *Collandra, Inc.*
2790 NW 104th Court
Miami, FL 33172
PHONE (800) 673-0532; FAX (305) 380-0859
WEB SITE   www.caribplace.com/foods/trout.htm
E-MAIL   colland@earthlink.net

Flying Fajitas
13710 Chittim Oak
San Antonio, TX 78232
PHONE (800) 290-3411
WEB SITE   www.fajitas.com; E-MAIL Flyingfajitas@stic.net

SIGNATURE PRODUCT   *Chicken and beef fajitas*

NEWEST PRODUCT   Mexican candy and Texas shaped chips
ADDITIONAL PRODUCTS   Mexican pralines; Texas chips and queso
(cheese dip); Texas "hot" peanuts; salsa; authentic guacamole; fresh
homemade flour tortillas; margarita mix; mexican "refried" beans;
fresh tomales

▦ *Yauco Selecto Estate Coffee*
595 Avenida Hostos
San Juan, PR 00918
PHONE (787) 782-0620; FAX (787) 767-8257
WEB SITE   www.yscoffee.com
E-MAIL   sales@yscoffee.com

GERMAN

▦ *La Vida Fina Bakery*
P.O. Box 34280
Bethesda, MD 20827-0280
PHONE (800) 229-4916
WEB SITE   http://www.his.com/~vidafina/
E-MAIL   vidafina@his.com

HAWAIIAN

All Hawaii Coffee
480 Kenolio Road #5-206
Kihei, HI 96753
PHONE (800) 565-2088; FAX (808) 875-4858
WEB SITE http://www.mauigateway.com/~coffee/
E-MAIL coffee@mauigateway.com

Lion Coffee
P.O. Box 1300, Lock Box #47867
Honolulu, HI 96813-5204
PHONE (800) 338-8353; FAX (800) 972-0777
WEB SITE www.lioncoffee.com
E-MAIL lion@lioncoffee.com

Mauna Loa Macadamia Nuts
6523 North Galena Road, P.O. Box 1772
Peoria, IL 61656
PHONE (800) 832-9993; FAX (309) 689-3893
WEB SITE www.maunaloa.com

INDIAN

Ethnic Tastes
470 Tripp Drive
Golden, CO 80401
PHONE (303) 271-0775; FAX (303) 271-0775
WEB SITE http://www.ethnic-tastes.com
E-MAIL mmisra@ethnic-tastes.com

SIGNATURE PRODUCT **Indian food, spices and groceries**

MEDITERRANEAN

3E Market

6753 Jones Mill Court, Suite A
Norcross, GA 30136
PHONE (800) 333-5548; FAX (800) 343-2652
WEB SITE http://www.3emarket.com
E-MAIL market@3e.com

SIGNATURE PRODUCT *Mediterranean Foods and Products*

ADDITIONAL PRODUCTS 3E Market brings you an enticing selection
  of Italian, Greek and other Mediterranean foods and products including oils, olives, pasta, sauces, biscotti and other specialty food items.
COMMENTS *These products are quite fun and good, a little bit non-stan-
  dard. I really liked the facaccia and the artichoke pate.*

Flying Noodle

1 Arrowhead Road
Duxbury, MA 02332
PHONE (800) 566-0599; FAX (617) 934-1527
WEB SITE www.flyingnoodle.com
E-MAIL bigparmesan@flyingnoodle.com

Furtado's

544 North Underwood
Fall River, MA 02720
PHONE (800) 845-4800; FAX (508) 679-5999

SIGNATURE PRODUCT *Portuguese sausage*

ADDITIONAL PRODUCTS Furtado's chourico and linguica available in
  patties, franks, and sausages

Manganaro Foods

488 Ninth Avenue
New York, NY 10018
PHONE (800) 4-SALAMI; FAX (212) 239-8355

SIGNATURE PRODUCT *Manganaro family cookbook*

ADDITIONAL PRODUCTS   A splendid line of good Italian products from
olive oils and vinegars, meats, cheeses, antipasto items, gift baskets to
espresso coffees. Also have an open-kitchen restaurant where cus-
tomers can eat . . . in the 104-year old store!
CATALOG INFO   Lovely black and white catalog
COMMENTS   *The cookbook is quite nice.*

 ### Pane e Salute

61 Central Street
Woodstock, VT 05091
PHONE (802) 457-4882

The Pasta Basket

P.O. Box 176
West Chester, OH 45071
PHONE (800) 759-8706; FAX (513) 777-8422
WEB SITE   www.pastabasket.com

Rossi Pasta Factory Inc.

114 Greene Street, P.O. Box 759
Marietta, OH 45750
PHONE (800) 227-6774; FAX (614) 373-5310
WEB SITE   www.civic.net/webmarket/ then select Rossi Pasta
E-MAIL   102121.2140@compuserve.com

Sultan's Delight

P.O. Box 090302
Brooklyn, NY 11209
PHONE (800) 852-5046; FAX (718) 745-2563

SIGNATURE PRODUCT *Mediterranean*

ADDITIONAL PRODUCTS   Fava beans, chick peas, bab gahannouj, fig
    jam, houmus, apricot jam pasta, pilaf, spices, rice, nuts, flower water,
    Turkish coffee and teas, sauces, olives, oils, halawa, filo dough, tahini,
    dried fruit and more

TECAPP srl

Lungotevere Flaminio 46
Rome ITALY 196
PHONE   ++396/321.51.15;   FAX   ++396/321.51.15
WEB SITE   http://www.italiantidbits.com
E-MAIL   e.romano@agora.stm.it

SIGNATURE PRODUCT *Italian and exotic tidbits*

ADDITIONAL PRODUCTS   All sort of Italian gourmet foods and special-
    ties like special biscuits, truffles, olive oil, botargo, pastas, the famous
    San Daniele ham and much more . . . exclusive and unique

▣ Termini Bros.

1523 South 8th Street
Philadelphia, PA 19147
PHONE (800) 882-7650; FAX (215) 334-0535
WEB SITE   www.termini.com

▣ Yasmin Gourmet Food

56 Pleasant Street
Greenville, RI 02828-1920
PHONE (401) 949-2121; FAX (401) 949-0991
WEB SITE   hudson.idt.net/~brbina19/
E-MAIL   bobbybina@hotmail.com

NORTHEASTERN

■ **Calef's Country Store**
Route 9, P.O. Box 57
Barrington, NH 03825
PHONE (603) 664-2231; FAX (603) 664-5857
WEB SITE   www.wertzcandy.com
E-MAIL   wertz@nbn.net

■ **The Joseph Cerniglia Winery**
37 West Road
Bennington, VT 5201
PHONE (800) 639-1625; FAX (802) 442-4410
WEB SITE   www.thisisvermont.com/vtwines.html
E-MAIL   grgrryan@sover.net

■ **Crowley Cheese**
Healdville Road
Healdville, VT 05758
PHONE (800) 683-2606; FAX (802) 259-2347

■ **Dakin Farm**
Route 7, RR1, Box 1775
Ferrisburg, VT 05456
PHONE (800) 993-2546; FAX (802) 425-2765
WEB SITE   www.dakinfarm.com
E-MAIL   dakin@vbimail.champlain.edu

■ **Daniel Weaver Company**
15th Avenue & Weavertown Road, P.O. Box 525
Lebanon, PA 17042
PHONE (800) WEAVERS; FAX (717) 274-6103

Foods of New York

66 Peconic Avenue
Medford, NY 11763
PHONE (800) HOTDOG-6; FAX (516) 654-9109
WEB SITE http://www.nyhotdog.com
E-MAIL steve@nyhotdog.com

SIGNATURE PRODUCT *Sabrett hot dogs; Gabila knishes; Drake's Cakes*

ADDITIONAL PRODUCTS We have created gift packages containing some or all of our products: Sabrett hot dogs, Gabila knishes, Drake's Cakes

Green Mountain Sugar House

Box 82, Route 100N
Ludlow, VT 05149
PHONE (800) 643-9338; FAX (802) 228-2298
E-MAIL gmsh@ludl.tds.net

Philly Food Division of Dial-A-Party Catering

107 S. Monroe Street
Media, PA 19063
PHONE (610) 565-4386; FAX (610) 566-8200
WEB SITE http://www.phillypretzels.com
E-MAIL philly@inet.net

SIGNATURE PRODUCT *Philly Cheese Steaks*

NEWEST PRODUCT Hot Roast Pork Sandwiches
ADDITIONAL PRODUCTS Made to order Philadelphia hoagies, freshly baked soft pretzels, Philadelphia scrapple, real Philly Italian sausage, sandwiches and Tastykakes.

Putnam Family Farm

RR 2, Box 2805
Cambridge, VT 05444.
PHONE (802) 644-2267; FAX (802) 644-6506
WEB SITE www.sover.net/~bputnam/index.htm
E-MAIL bputnam@sover.net

▦ Wood's Cider Mill
RFD #2, Box 477
Springfield, VT 05156
PHONE (802) 263-5547

NORTHWESTERN

▦ Tillamook Cheese
4175 Highway 101 N, P.O. Box 313
Tillamook, OR 97141
PHONE (800) 542-7290; FAX (503) 815-1305

▦ The Children's Catalog
Children's Home Society of Washington, P.O. Box 15190
Seattle, WA 98115
PHONE (800) 856-5437; FAX (206) 523-1667
WEB SITE www.chs-wa.org

ORIENTAL

Krua Thai
1106 Littlepage Street
Fredericksburg, VA 22401
PHONE (540) 374-9362; FAX (540) 374-9362
WEB SITE http://www.thaitar.com
E-MAIL kruathai@thaitara.com

SIGNATURE PRODUCT **Thai Gourmet Dinner Kits**

NEWEST PRODUCT Gourmet gift sets (e.g. rice varieties selection; coming soon: herbal vinegar kit with recipes, bottled seeds)

ADDITIONAL PRODUCTS   We specialize in Thai menu kits; supplying spices, all hard to find ingredients, full instructions and our own special recipes — anything to make cooking Thai cuisine fun and flavorful.

COMMENTS   *These are fantastic, very authentic products. The dinner kit was truly a great, fun way to have a Thai meal, it's a real EVENT! This is on my "must try" list.*

The Oriental Pantry

423 Great Road
Acton, MA 01720
PHONE (800) 828-0368; FAX (617) 275-4506
WEB SITE   www.orientalpantry.com
E-MAIL   oriental@orientalpantry.com

SIGNATURE PRODUCT   **Asian foods**

ADDITIONAL PRODUCTS   Many hard-to-find oriental spices, sauces, oils, teas, noodles, vegetables, wine, snacks, relishes, chutney, curry, nuts and seeds, fresh ginger and lemon grass, dressings, fortune cookies, cookbooks and cooking accessories

Spice Merchant

P.O. Box 524
Jackson Hole, WY 83001
PHONE (800) 551-5999; FAX (307) 733-6343
WEB SITE   emall.com/spke
E-MAIL   71553.436@compuserve.con

SIGNATURE PRODUCT   **Oriental goods**

ADDITIONAL PRODUCTS   Extensive line of Chinese, Japanese, Thai and Indonesian sauces, condiments, spices, and dried foods

CATALOG INFO   Includes many cooking utensils and specialty items necessary for Oriental cooking — extensive

Wakagiya Yoshiyasu USA
3833-138th Avenue SE
Bellevue, WA 98006
PHONE (425) 562-8869; FAX (425) 562-8869
WEB SITE http://www.wagashi.com
E-MAIL wakagiya@wagashi.com

SIGNATURE PRODUCT *Otezumemonaka*

NEWEST PRODUCT Seasonal Assorted Higashi
ADDITIONAL PRODUCTS Ohagi Tsubuan and Shirotsubuan
Kinakomochi Kusamochi

SCANDINAVIAN

Nordic House
3421 Telegraph Avenue
Oakland, CA 94609
PHONE (800) 854-6435; FAX (510) 653-1936
WEB SITE nordichouse.com
E-MAIL pia@nordichouse.com

SIGNATURE PRODUCT *Scandinavian food*

ADDITIONAL PRODUCTS Candies, breads, cheeses, pickled fish,
seafood, meat, cookbooks, and cookware

O & H Danish Bakery
1841 Douglas Avenue
Racine, WI 53402
PHONE (800) 227-6665; FAX (414) 637-4215
WEB SITE www.bakery.com/oh.danish.kringle
E-MAIL ohdanish@wi.net

SOUTHERN

▨ *Bland Farms*
P.O. Box 506-PG19
Glenndale, GA 30427
PHONE (800) 843-2542; FAX (912) 654-1330
WEB SITE www.blandfarms.com

▨ *Blood's Hammock Groves*
4600 Linton Boulevard
Delray Beach, FL 33445
PHONE (800) 255-5188; FAX (561) 498-0285
WEB SITE www.bhgcitrus.com
E-MAIL blood's@bhgcitrus.com

Callaway Gardens

P.O. Box 2000
Pine Mountain, GA 31822-2000
PHONE (800) 280-7524; FAX (706) 663-5058

SIGNATURE PRODUCT *Muscadine preserves*

ADDITIONAL PRODUCTS Muscadine sauce, jellies, jams, vidalia onion
gift box, hams, speckled heart grits, and much more
CATALOG INFO The catalog is very nice with many interesting items.
COMMENTS *The grits were really terrific and a nice item for this Northerner
to get from a "real" Southern outfit.*

▨ *Florida Fruit Shippers*
5006 Gulfport Boulevard S
Gulfport, FL 33707
PHONE (800) 715-8279; FAX (813) 323-5412
WEB SITE www.orangesonline.com
E-MAIL ffs@orangesonline

Rowena's
758 West 22nd Street
Norfolk, VA 23517
PHONE (800) 627-8699; FAX (804) 627-1505
WEB SITE pilotonline.com/Rowena's
E-MAIL Rowena's@aol.com

Virginia Diner
P.O. Box 1030
Wakefield, VA 23888
PHONE (800) 868-6887; FAX (757) 899-2281
WEB SITE www.vadiner.com
E-MAIL vadiner@infi.net

SOUTHWESTERN

Bluebonnet Gourmet
P.O. Box 132145
Tyler, TX 75712-2145
PHONE (800) 657-1895; FAX (903) 509-8000
WEB SITE www.bluebonnetgourmet.com
E-MAIL blubonet@gower.net

Jane Butel's Pecos Valley Spice
2429 Monroe Street, N.E.
Albuquerque, NM 87110
PHONE (800) 473-TACO; FAX (505) 888-4269

SIGNATURE PRODUCT **Mexican/Southwestern products**

ADDITIONAL PRODUCTS Tacos, tortillas, chiles, chili kits, whole chile pods, spices, beans, barbecue, videos, cookbooks, kitchen essentials for Mexican and Southwestern cooking

The Gourmet Trading Company

1071 Avenida Acaso
Camarillo, CA 93012
PHONE (800) 888-3484; FAX (805) 389-4790
WEB SITE www.gourmettrader.com; E-MAIL trader@gourmettrader.com

SIGNATURE PRODUCT **Southwestern Foods**

ADDITIONAL PRODUCTS Gourmet chili fixin's, salsa, hot sauces, homemade pasta, organic pasta sauces, spiced olives, infused olive oil, vinegars, marinades, BBQ sauce, mustards, herbs & spices, kitchenware and more

COMMENTS *The XXX Hot Salsa Habanero was very good; not too, too!*

Los Chileros de Nuevo Mexico

P.O. Box 6215
Sante Fe, NM 87502
PHONE (505) 471-6967; FAX (505) 473-7306
WEB SITE www.hotchilepepper.com/ordering.htm

SIGNATURE PRODUCT **Los chileros**

NEWEST PRODUCT Salsa mix

ADDITIONAL PRODUCTS Exotic chiles, blue corn products, New Mexico chiles, various white and yellow corn products

COMMENTS *These are wonderful products, beautifully packaged with good recipes. I fried the sopaipilla mix into tortillas and every one wanted more. Muy bueno and on my "must try" list.*

Miguel's Stowe Away

RR3, Box 2086
Waterbury, VT 05676
PHONE (800) 448-6517; FAX (802) 244-7804
E-MAIL miguels@together.net

Santa Fe Select

410 Old Santa Fe Trail
Santa Fe, NM 87501
PHONE (800) 243-0353

Sierra Sunset Inc.

P.O. Box 525
Crugers, NY 10522
PHONE (800) 832-8990; FAX (914) 739-7541
WEB SITE usa-web.com/drinks/margarita
E-MAIL sierrasunset-mchang@worldnet.att.net

SIGNATURE PRODUCT **Fruit juice blend for margarita**

NEWEST PRODUCT Chili pepper spice
COMMENTS *Their products remind me of the great times living in Mexico. Terrific!*

 ### Sphinx Date Ranch

3039 N. Scottsdale Road
Scottsdale, AZ 85251
PHONE (800) 482-3283; FAX (602) 941-1840
WEB SITE calzona.com/sphinx
E-MAIL sphinx@infinet.rs.com

Superbly Southwestern

2400 Rio Grande NW #1-171
Albuquerque, NM 87104
PHONE (800) 467-4HOT
WEB SITE www.hotchile.com
E-MAIL hotchile@aol.com

SIGNATURE PRODUCT **New Mexico green chile**

ADDITIONAL PRODUCTS Salsas, sauces, dips, red chile, Southwestern mixes. And green chile: fresh, frozen or bottled.
COMMENTS *The green chile was VERY HOT, even the mild was spicy; but authentic!*

INDEX